BEYOND DEATH
AND DISHONOUR

BEYOND DEATH AND DISHONOUR

One Japanese at War in New Zealand

Michiharu Shinya

Translated by Eric H. Thompson

Castle

CASTLE PUBLISHING
AUCKLAND
NEW ZEALAND

Beyond Death and Dishonour

Published by Castle Publishing Ltd

PO Box 68-800 Newton,

Auckland, New Zealand

Phone: +64-9-378 4052

Fax: +64-9-376 3855

ISBN 0-9582124-6-5

Originally published as *The Path from Guadalcanal* 0-908571-27-5

by Outrigger Publishers, Auckland, New Zealand

© 1979, Original translation from Japanese by Eric Hardisty Thompson

© 1988, Published in Japan by Seibunsha Publishing as *From the Sea of Death to the Pulpit*

Text revised for this edition by Kay Wall

Editor: Vivienne Hill

Production: Andrew Killick

Cover design by Jeff Hagan

Printed in New Zealand by Wentforth Print, Auckland

Cover photo: Michiharu Shinya (1937) (courtesy of the author)

I dedicate this book
to the people of New Zealand with my deep thanks.

Michiharu Shinya

Out of the depths I cry to you, O LORD.

Psalm 130:1

Acknowledgements

I wish to extend my deepest thanks to all those involved in this project, in particular my friend Eric H Thompson who originally translated this book, and who sadly passed away last year. I would also like to thank Kay Wall for her revision of the book, the staff of Castle Publishing in New Zealand for producing this new edition, all those who encouraged me to write my story, and OMF International for their support.

Thanks to Robert and Alison Smith, Warren and Doreen Payne, and Capt. Nigel Luscombe for their advice and input on aspects of the text. Thanks to Stewart Hillman for proofreading and encouragement.

Thanks to Noel Earles, and the Alexander Turnbull Library, National Library of New Zealand, Te Puna Matauranga o Aotearoa for kindly allowing us to use their photographs.

Lastly I would like to thank my wife and family, and God who saved me in my darkest hour.

Contents

1

Guadalcanal

Guadalcanal loomed to starboard, close and ominous through the pervading blackness. Moment by moment we were pressing closer to enemy territory. On the Japanese destroyer *Akatsuki*'s darkened bridge nerves were taut and all were concentrated on lookout.

It was just past midnight, 13 November 1942. I was a naval lieutenant, serving as torpedo officer on the destroyer *Akatsuki*—an escort for the Guadalcanal Volunteer Force. I gave the preliminary orders to prepare our torpedoes and stood at the starboard firing control position, ready to launch. Would the enemy fleet be ready and waiting? Yesterday an American B-17 reconnaissance plane had spotted us. Our fighters had failed to destroy it so it seemed our hopes of a surprise attack fled with the pilot.

Our commander in chief, Yamamoto, had established his headquarters at Truk, the linchpin of Japan's naval defence, to better control operations. Truk provided a perfect staging base to support Rabaul, 1500 kms south. Ships based at Rabaul could strike quickly at any point in the Solomons or New Guinea. From our air bases there, we could bomb targets as distant as Darwin, Australia.

The strategy adopted from Truk was to use a battleship squadron to gain mastery of the Guadalcanal airfield. It was vital that we expelled the Americans and controlled our airfield again. Whoever controlled the airfield controlled Guadalcanal. In turn, whoever controlled Guadalcanal controlled the Solomon Islands, a chain approximately 800 kms long. The American occupation threatened our air bases at Rabaul and thus was a menace to all Japanese operations in the area.

The battleships of the Eleventh Squadron, *Hiei* and *Kirishima*, under Vice Admiral Hiroaki Abe, would pound the enemy at the airfield with their 36 cm main guns at midnight, 12 November. With a shortage of destroyers at Truk, *Akatsuki* was chosen to be one of the escorts for the battleship squadron. The main strength of the Second Fleet, commanded by Vice Admiral Nobutake Kondo, together with the aircraft carrier *Jun'yo* would provide support.

If the enemy were alerted, our advance destroyer division would forewarn us. Our hearing strained to pick up the slightest crackle from the radiotelephone, but no interruption came.

The Americans were at last recovering from the rout of Pearl Harbour and had inflicted their first real counter-attack with their bold landing on the island on the 7 August. Japanese construction units had completed the airfield and our planes were about to occupy the base when it was snatched away, leaving us looking like a man who's had his fried bean curd stolen by a scavenging hawk.

Critical battles were fought in and around Guadalcanal in the Solomon Islands over six months from August 1942. Some 30,000 Japanese died in these campaigns. American deaths were fewer but for all participants, Guadalcanal became known as a hellhole of jungle warfare and tropical disease.

Land-based air power was superior to sea-based air power. An enemy fleet operating in a zone controlled by friendly land-based bombers, risked huge losses. Japanese occupation of the Solomons could provide a springboard for further operations against the supply line between the United States and Australia. Supplies allowed one to make war and kept armies alive. Armies without supplies faced the jungle alone and, in the South Pacific, the jungle killed. Therefore the Americans had to be ejected.

We felt confident that Guadalcanal would be re-taken once our army launched a general offensive. This previously obscure island, lying at the south-eastern end of the Solomons group, now came to the forefront as a battlefield; a Seki-ga-hara of the Pacific war. The enemy controlled the air although we still controlled part of the island.

"Something spotted—looks like enemy," called the lookout. Nerves already taut, tightened further.

Almost immediately the radiotelephone crackled. "Enemy sighted." Our original plan for bombardment of the airfield by the two battleships dissolved. The commanding officer of the Destroyer Division and the ship's captain frantically reassessed their tactics. Through my torpedo-aiming telescope, I saw several faint black silhouettes loom into view.

Suddenly one turned towards us, approaching rapidly. From a careful examination it seemed to be an enemy destroyer, and extraordinarily close. As it came opposite our starboard beam, I identified it as an enemy single-funnelled destroyer of the newer type. We guessed that it was probably the advance patrol for the enemy's main body.

Darkness gave us an edge. Our navy was well trained in night-battle and possessed superior optics and oxygen-propelled torpedoes. These were more powerful, faster and of longer range than those of any other navy. A major disadvantage was that we had no radar; therefore we had to switch on searchlights before firing our night gunnery.

Should we carry on past, or should we attack? Had they noticed us? Bite, or get bitten? Pre-battle tension heightened as adrenaline flowed but found no release.

The commanding officer ordered us to confirm the destroyer's identity.

"Enemy—no mistake, Sir!" I snapped. Several menacing profiles lurked to starboard. It seemed prudent to quietly let the destroyer pass and save our attack for the cruisers ahead.

The commanding officer decided otherwise.

"Fire!" he barked to the upper gunnery control position. The gun turrets swung round. An instant later a searchlight skewered the enemy destroyer in the darkness. We'd taken that final step, the moment of battle in which we revealed our position. Only a pause to hold one's breath before the first shot was fired...

I thought, surely now...

BANG! ! !

A deafening thunder followed a blinding flash. The deck shook violently and a blast of pressure knocked me down. "We're hit." I reacted instinctively.

So now it's my turn to die! I thought. For a moment I felt drawn far away, my mind captured by a quiet and distant sensation. But then it seemed I was not dead at all. "What the hell?" I mumbled.

I struggled to sit up, surprised that I could. My head rang and my right cheek felt hot. Blood trickled from my forehead into my right eye while, shell-shocked, I stared vacantly.

It took only one instant to shatter the boundary between sanity and insanity. Cool reason fled, capacity for thought disappeared and animal instinct took over. I lost self-awareness in a kind of delirium. In the darkness I had no idea of the extent of my wounds. Though still alive, I had a sense of impending death.

The commanding officer swung around and ordered, "Port the helm." I realised the helmsman was no longer beside me. Sitting, I tried to turn the helm but the wheel spun uselessly. "She's not responding," I replied. In slow motion, I managed to stand. All the men near me lay motionless. Only the commanding officer, the captain, the navigating officer, the assistant navigating officer and I were left alive on the bridge. I noticed my cap was gone and my shoes had disappeared. Blood streamed across the deck. My socks soaked it up and stuck to the soles of my feet.

The commanding officer tried to contact the upper gunnery control position but there was no response.

The acrid stench of explosives burnt my throat. Even in the darkness I knew that the bridge instruments had suffered massive damage. When I looked to the rear, all the men lay lifeless. The entire firing section of the torpedo department, except me, had been wiped out. The destroyer division's medical officer and paymaster were also dead.

The shell had probably come from one of the ships on the starboard bow and had struck the rear of the bridge. All vital systems defunct, control had been lost over the entire ship.

Casualties were not limited to the bridge. Someone soon came with a report that a shell had hit the starboard engine room. *Akatsuki* could no longer hold its course. Acting on instinct, I set off to try to man the auxiliary steering gear at the stern.

A dead body blocked the hatch, slowing me down. As I descended the narrow ladder into darkness, the signal room could be seen through its half-open door; several signalmen sat in position, motionless. At the bottom of the ladder I glanced into the wardroom. During battle this became a medical treatment room. The scene was worse than I'd expected. Many wounded were already laid out while more arrived from the ship's aft. Dim candlelight threw eerie shadows over the wounded and dying.

Bright red flames flared from the No.1 boiler room towards the stern. Why go on? I thought, tempted to give up.

Blood trickling into my eye hindered my efforts so I allowed a medical orderly to fit a makeshift headband. As if sleepwalking, I returned to the bridge.

The port engine room must also have been damaged and the ship, like a creature with its legs torn off, now drifted helplessly. An enemy destroyer raced past. The commanding officer ordered me to establish contact with the engine rooms, but I raised no response. The captain and the navigating officer just stood in position, silent. Our situation was hopeless. I wondered where the assistant navigating officer had gone.

Akatsuki had been left behind in hostile waters while the battle shifted further to the west.

With water flooding in, the ship began to go down, listing to port. As she sank deeper, the list slowly increased. Only three of us remained on the bridge: the captain, the navigating officer and myself. The commanding officer must have been elsewhere. No one spoke. The tilt increased until we could no longer stand erect, but propped ourselves against the ship's compass. The flames from the fire in the No.1 boiler room had steadily grown to envelop the whole bridge from behind.

At length the list became so great that we were forced to cling to the window frames. The sea loomed up before us and we finally leapt off.

I watched the bridge sink below the surface. *Akatsuki* raised her bow as she lay on her port side, then gently disappeared. Nothing remained but the quiet sea.

I'd heard how a sinking ship sucked survivors below water and so knew what to expect. Several seconds passed and I imagined that perhaps we wouldn't be dragged under. But then a tremendous force suddenly pulled me down into the abyss. I had no idea how far, or in what direction. I had absolutely no feeling of life and sensed only pitch-blackness. Struggling seemed pointless and I resigned myself to the outcome.

On the way down I heard a dull belly-shaking explosion; possibly one of the depth charges with its safety catch released had exploded, but I couldn't be sure. Lungs aching, I involuntarily gulped some water. This revived me a little but unless I reached air, all would be over.

At last the will to resist kicked in and I struggled upwards. Lack of air again forced me to choke on water. When would I ever reach the surface?

Suddenly my head broke through. The water still surged in the aftermath of the ship's sinking. I gasped so eagerly for breath that water mingled with air and brought on a fit of coughing and spluttering.

Soon I noticed the heads of others and the survivors began calling to each other. We groped for floating spars, carried for emergencies.

Our ships seemed to have turned back and the fighting had shifted towards Savo Island. The star shells fired by the Americans burst beautifully in the dark sky, their blue-white light reflected brightly against the sea. It was an awesome fireworks display. Occasionally shells whistled past nearby, trailing an unearthly moaning sound.

Of all the dramas performed on the human stage, the spectacle of battle is without equal; the devil that lurks in human nature whispers encouragement. Dishing it out offers the best perspective, while being on the receiving end is unbearable. For nearly a year I had been participating in the war, a victor watching the vanquished.

Now my turn had come to experience the harsh realities. In due time the guns fell quiet. Darkness and silence enveloped me. I was left behind, alone in the sea, clinging to my driftwood.

2

Taken Prisoner

Almost imperceptibly the darkness began to fade, losing intensity in stages, until I could see the heads of men dotting the ocean. As night receded, Guadalcanal Island slept on in deep silence. I swam towards the beach still held by our army.

A new morning, the 13th day of November. In just one night I experienced a sudden reversal of fortune, an abrupt change of circumstance and identity. My mind struggled to get a grip on reality. I felt like I was in a dream.

The placid water supported a scattering of thirty to forty men. I recognised every face; they were all *Akatsuki* crew. I wondered what had happened to the captain and the navigating officer. I scanned the sea but perhaps they perished when we'd been sucked beneath the water. As far as I could tell, the *Akatsuki* appeared to be the only casualty of the night's battle, which helped boost my confidence. As the sun rose, the surrounding islands showed up more brightly.

Among the survivors, some men were relatively unhurt while others were badly affected. A petty officer from my section was in a critical condition. I did my best to get him onto a fairly wide plank and kept an eye on him as I swam. He was weak, his face pale. The Japanese-held shore shimmered in the distance. The sun rose over Guadalcanal and shone directly on our heads.

A droning engine abruptly shattered the peace. As I glanced around, I saw a small American landing craft heading straight towards us. For a moment I was not worried and dismissed it. But in a flash I understood they were coming to collect us. "That's done it!" I blurted out loud, "Our carelessness means we'll be taken prisoner." This above everything we Japanese fighting men traditionally regarded as the most unbearable shame. To become a captive of the enemy now threatened. My mind spun.

Shaken, I realised it was dangerous for us to be bunched together. To avoid capture we swam off in different directions, ever further apart.

Another landing craft went past at high speed, so close that I saw the faces of the American sailors. The wake tossed me about and I spluttered as I swallowed water. If this is how things are, I thought, I'd be better off dead. In the distance I could see them picking up our men. Panicking, I again tried to swim as far away as possible.

The landing craft disappeared into the distance and with the crisis over my agitated mind began to quieten.

The few of us remaining were now more scattered, mere unrecognisable dots on the ocean. Due to our evasive action, the shore was even further off and I wondered if it would be possible to reach it before evening.

Little strength remained; 'swimming' only loosely defined my feeble efforts. I held my direction and swam toward shore noting my position relative to the land. It never changed in the least. Maybe it was my imagination, but at times I wondered whether the tide carried me backwards. Nonetheless, my destination remained in sight and I hoped that somehow I'd reach it before night. Even in such a hopeless situation a person can be surprisingly calm.

Guadalcanal spread before me, a continuous dense jungle presenting a face of utter indifference to warring humanity. Away to the west, Savo Island stood out distinctly. Far to the north, the island of Florida spread low and hazy.

I became aware of an enemy cruiser of the 10,000 ton *Augusta* class, I paused. It drifted between our army and me, blocking my way. My exhausted body couldn't keep up with my overwrought spirit. While my arms and legs twitched feebly, in my imagination I surged ahead to the safe shore.

Suddenly the forward gun turrets of the cruiser belched flame, rending the air with a thunderclap. Perhaps some of our ships still fought on the far side of Savo Island? The forward 8 inch guns fired a few salvos then fell silent. Tranquillity returned. Careful scrutiny showed that the cruiser's

No.3 rear turret had been damaged, probably from last night's battle. Such evidence that the enemy had not emerged unscathed brought me some satisfaction.

In due time the cruiser quietly slipped away and began circling. The fact that it periodically blocked my direction left me at a loss. Sometimes it came so close that I could distinguish the figures of the crew. The small Stars and Stripes flag waving from the rear may have been much faded by sea air, but it represented an unbearable threat as I drifted. Woe indeed to the vanquished!

As time passed the sea became lukewarm and the surface increasingly leaden. The sun rose higher, rays beating mercilessly on my head. I had no idea how much time had passed. I dipped my head in the water to cool off but it didn't make much difference. To make matters worse, heavy oil coated my entire body. The salt water stung my eyes and for long periods I couldn't open them. My ears rang incessantly while my head wounds, coupled with scattered wits, caused concern. A nasty gash on my right hand had turned a hideous colour. Despair settled upon me.

Adding to my discomfort, I must have swallowed some oil, which gave me several bad bouts of diarrhoea. My intestines bloated and I floated limply, every scrap of strength drained from my body. Weak reflexive movements kept me up. I could not sustain this activity for long and often lay on my back to rest. The possibility of death held no fears.

I looked ahead, half-heartedly. Two ship-based floatplanes from the cruiser had alighted on the water while the ship had moved well out to sea. Without realising, I'd got so close to one of them that I could distinguish the pilot's head. "Stupid!" I muttered, and started to swim away. Meanwhile, the other took off and climbed away.

Suddenly a strange buzzing arrived overhead and I glanced up as the plane swooped towards me. I'll collect it this time, I thought, expecting the rat-tat-tat of a machine-gun. But no such thing happened; the plane swung its nose away and peace returned. I couldn't understand what he was up to why would he pick out a man floating alone in the sea.

Then it happened again; buzzing, followed by diving. Just as I expected the machine-gun rattle, the plane's nose lifted and he flew off. Only then I realised that the pilot was indicating my position to someone else. I stiffened and stole a fearful glance to the east. I'm done for, I thought.

A small landing craft headed my way from where the other plane had alighted. My heart thumped, I felt confused and my vision was hazy.

An impulse to fade from existence seized me, to simply disappear beneath the water, but I couldn't even manage that. It's no use, I thought, cornered like a mouse stalked by a cat. The landing craft came closer...

The sound of the engine was right behind me, and then voices. I assumed an attitude of indifference but couldn't resist turning to look. Two sailors reached down to pick me up.

"No thanks!" I blurted in English. My paramount duty was loyalty, even at the cost of my life. As the Emperor Meiji's Imperial Rescript states: 'Duty is weightier than a mountain while death is lighter than a feather.'

I tried to move away but my fragile condition, combined with decreased mobility in water, made resistance ineffective. You must fight to the last, I thought. But the realisation hit me that however much I struggled, in this situation it would make no difference. In the end they grabbed me and heaved me on board.

How much I would later berate myself for that moment. Why didn't you resist to the last? It was your duty! It's easy to be wise after the event.

In the boat my knees gave way and I collapsed. Buoyancy had supported me whilst in the sea, but with that removed, I lay helpless. I was surprised to see four or five men from our ship already squatting in the boat. My pitiful state shamed me and I said nothing. I marvelled at how quickly my fortunes had changed.

My naval career had started back in August 1940. I had graduated from the Naval Academy and served a period as crewmember of the cruiser *Katori* of the training squadron. This was followed by half a year on the 10,000 ton cruiser *Nachi* as aide to the captain and lookout duties. At the beginning of the Pacific war I was signals and navigating officer on the destroyer *Amagiri* of the 20th Destroyer Division, and had taken part in operations in Malaya, French Indo–China, Sumatra and Indian Ocean theatres of war. Once these 'first-stage' operations were successfully concluded, we returned home. There I attended a course at the Yokosuka Torpedo School for ships officers. I then transferred to the *Akatsuki* in May. Now I realised my life would never be the same.

After a while I became aware that the engine had stopped; the speed declined rapidly until the boat bumped onto the beach. Tall coconut palms pressed close to the shore. We had landed far to the east, beyond Lunga Point. For the first time I saw many American soldiers close up. Before their gaze, my humiliation as one of the defeated made me shudder.

Ordered onto a large truck nearby, we struggled to walk, barely able to lift our feet. Once loaded, the truck started off and soon arrived in a compound enclosed by crude barbed wire fencing.

The compound consisted of two divisions; one already held some ten or more men from *Akatsuki*. Standing proved too much for me and I slumped to the ground. My coating of sticky oil made matters worse and shell splinters had torn my hands and legs leaving raw, open wounds. My head hammered while my dazed state left me wondering whether or not it was me in my body.

Later, someone, apparently an enemy medical orderly, examined each of us and applied dressings to our wounds. We just let him do it. No longer fighting men, we resembled beggars or refugees.

By now the sunlight slanted through the coconut palms so I figured I must have been captured about noon. Even thinking required a supreme effort. I sprawled on the ground with a blanket over my head, overcome by a languid drowsiness, and soon fell into a deep sleep.

In the middle of a pleasant and peaceful dream about my homeland, I abruptly woke in half-light. Sailors slept beside me on the ground. For a moment complete confusion reigned. I came to with a start as the bitter realisation of my plight struck. Could I have been taken prisoner? This notion turned my dream into a nightmare.

In the morning the ground was chilled and the air cool, but as the sun rose the cruel tropical heat returned.

The seriously wounded occupied one half of the compound. We were housed under a crudely built rectangular shelter, floor slightly raised and sides open to the air. The other half, where we lay, contained an American military tent, a simple cookhouse and an open-air latrine. The perimeter fence was incomplete and not very high. If anyone had wanted to escape, it wouldn't have presented much of a challenge, but the jungle beyond was an effective deterrent.

It seemed to me that the American troops lived a fairly comfortable life. The quality of their equipment surprised me—their unfamiliar steel helmets, automatic rifles and well-fitting uniforms. They showed no signs of being the unkempt, ill-disciplined, inferior troops our superiors had portrayed.

During our second night we heard the booming thunder of guns coming from the sea around Savo Island.

For two or three days I couldn't sort out or control my feelings at all. Events since the sinking kept spinning bewilderingly round my head.

I spent my days in a dream-like trance, hoping that soon I'd wake up and find myself free. The thought that I'd been taken prisoner threatened my whole being and mingled with a strong urge to resist captivity. It took some time before I accepted that I'd become a Prisoner-of-War. For a few days I was so tired that I slept almost constantly, lying wrapped in a blanket. Mental turmoil accompanied any waking moments.

During this period several men died. A petty officer from my section had nothing wrong externally, but he couldn't hold out long against an internal haemorrhage. His dead body lay on the ground, tightly wrapped in a blanket, jet-black with a swarm of flies drawn by the stench of death. Was this the final condition of Man, the lord of creation? I had taken part in the war, witnessing its tragedies often enough, but I felt keenly the death of this man I'd served with. On the other hand, one could only be envious of a man able to die like this with no great suffering.

Guadalcanal was on the front line between the armies of Japan and America; hostile feelings were strong on both sides and blood was up. In many ways the Americans' position remained insecure and their attitude reflected this.

The sergeant in charge was a strongly built man with a florid face and a fierce countenance. Endowed with a villainous character, his rigid features seemed to match his humourless personality. He periodically sauntered amongst us during the day, usually naked from the waist up, displaying coloured tattoos in the middle of his chest and on both arms. There was even a Japanese geisha amongst them. As a member of the Marine Corps he had probably visited the Orient. A sharp jungle knife always hung at his waist.

Our meals consisted of supplies left behind by Japanese construction units when the Americans captured the base: unpalatable dried vegetables, bean paste, wheat flour and rice. Not that I had much appetite anyway.

As POWs, we were no longer a unit of the Japanese armed forces. The hierarchy of command broke down and intuition guided each of us. We were just individual men or, more appropriately, instinctive animals. It was alarming how quickly the change occurred.

A burning thirst constantly gripped me but the water was muddy and almost undrinkable. I also developed a craving for fruit, thinking I might never taste it again before dying.

For several days I lay in the tent and never wanted to get up. During the night my head ached continuously. My ears throbbed and oozed pus; however often I wiped them with paper it kept flowing. Daytime saw countless flies swarming at the open wounds in my ears, hands and legs. Even in this state, I could not willingly accept help. Was it fitting that a man who must die—a man so disgraced by capture—should receive medical treatment? Conflict raged in my mind.

Enemy planes bearing the star insignia swept low over the compound where we lay. Coconut trees blocked our view on all sides but it seemed certain that the airfield was close. From evening to morning things were quiet but as soon as dawn broke, the noise of engines burst from the airfield and a continuous procession of planes arrived and departed.

A few days after our capture two young airmen were also incarcerated. They were the only survivors from a land-based medium attack bomber shot down at sea.

Days passed and in my muddled state events gradually fell into place and a sense of reality returned. This forced me to face the truth that I *had* become a POW. For this I reproached myself bitterly.

In the Japanese armed forces we respected one principle above all others:whatever happened, the enemy would never capture us. We made this our particular pride, a contrast to the forces of every other country. Die, but never become a POW. This intrinsic doctrine shaped the traditional beliefs of our fighting men—doubting it never occurred to us. To become a POW was the ultimate disgrace and a serious crime deserving no less than death. Though still living in the flesh, I could no longer live in Japanese society. My life as good as ended when the Americans plucked me from the water.

A tormenting voice continually accused, "Did you really fight to the very end?" Another voice replied, "No. You gave up. If any proof is needed, aren't you alive here now, among the enemy?" Somehow I had to put an immediate end to this condition. I considered escaping alone at night. But there would have been little chance of success and it seemed improper to separate from the others.

Another plan occurred to me. I casually mentioned to a couple of men, "What if we all fight them with our bare hands. If we do it a couple of times, we'll all be able to die." Each one told me that there would be some other occasion to die, sometime later. Naively, I'd thought that I'd find death alongside the others. What a weak way of thinking, worthy of an insect. One must die alone.

Eventually I came to realise that the enlisted men were, after all, hardly to blame. Hadn't they been taken prisoner through no fault of their own? I didn't know what would happen to them, but shouldn't I go along and take responsibility? I soon rejected that idea. As far as I was concerned, only by dying could I show the best way out for them.

After labouring through all these thoughts, I felt cursed by my helpless nature. I reached my final resolution: I must die—but how?

Until now I'd assumed that in a crisis a man would simply be able to kill himself. My situation proved otherwise. When I came to grips with the problem, I discovered that a powerful instinct for life lurked within, an insidious traitor, urging me to stay alive. It had worked covertly through the recent battle and now controlled me. Daily the conflict racked my mind; a sense of humiliation and guilt hounded me.

The enlisted men appeared relatively indifferent to the officers' plight. Of course they suffered too, but perhaps they had a sense of reliance and assurance from the men of higher or equal rank. The weight of my position as an officer caused deep anguish. I was barely 22-years-old, unworldly, purely and simply loving Japan, having lived only that I could die for my country.

A few days after the arrival of the airmen, we awoke to find they'd disappeared. The demon sergeant strode in scowling and lined us up outside the tent. After a head count, the MPs mustered and a search began. They brought several large police dogs with them and, as if from nowhere, some of the natives turned out to assist in the search.

Eventually four American soldiers came into our enclosure carrying a stretcher. We couldn't see who it was as they took him into the neighbouring area. The sergeant appeared and became furious when he discovered it was one of the escapees. He flung himself at the man, beating him in a rain of fists. That day or the next more punishment ensued. The airman dug pits and was forced to stand for long hours in the blazing sun. They even pretended they were going to shoot him, to add psychological torment to physical. We never saw the other escapee again and could only guess his fate.

As day followed day, my inner war continued. I stayed vigilant, hoping for a change in circumstances and a chance to die. I knew we would eventually be transferred elsewhere, and I looked forward expectantly.

How many days had passed since my internment? I had lost any correct sense of time and could not tell which day of November it was. We had probably spent more than ten days in this compound when at last the day came to leave Guadalcanal.

3
Shipped Away

One afternoon a large truck drove into our enclosure. With no forewarning we found ourselves being hustled up onto it at the orders of several military policemen. Of course we had no idea where we were being taken, but wherever it might be, I was glad to be leaving the compound.

The truck drove out and stopped at the shore. There were many enemy soldiers in fatigue uniforms on the beach; some looked at us blankly, while others gazed on us as rarities.

Between the island of Florida and Guadalcanal, the wide stretch of sea lay utterly calm. It was hard to believe that this was the scene of fierce battles between Japanese and American forces. A freighter now anchored there, and further offshore a destroyer stood guard. Several landing craft plied between ship and shore, apparently unloading supplies and materials. Large netting sacks of potatoes had been thrown on the beach, and my eye caught the trademark 'California' written across them.

Before long we shuffled into a large empty landing craft and headed for the freighter. After struggling up the long swaying gangway they lined us up along the deck on one side of the ship. One of their medical officers gave us a brief physical inspection to ascertain the extent of our wounds. Then we were taken down to one of the ship's forward holds as the unloading was completed.

The interior was empty except for some twenty or more mattresses, one for each of us. These had been spread across the wide concrete floor.

We stretched out on these mattresses—broken men. It felt like being at the bottom of a well; far above at the upper-deck level we could glimpse the blue sky through the square hatch opening. A steel wall without a single opening enclosed us and only one slender steel ladder gave access to the deck above.

As I lay there all sorts of imaginings galloped and wheeled through my head. Would we be going to the American mainland, or perhaps some other country? I remembered Kazuo Sakamaki, my classmate of Naval Academy days. He had failed in the midget submarine attack on Pearl Harbour at the beginning of the war and had been taken prisoner. I now felt some affinity with him. Would he be still alive? Surely a man like him would not keep on living after being taken prisoner? It's the ones like me who are so contemptible. I flinched at the harsh inner voice of scorn.

The next day the ship weighed anchor and got under way. When they opened the hatch, bright sunlight shone upon us. I used my intuition to determine the angle of the sun's rays, trying to judge the general direction the ship was taking, but wasn't very successful.

Soon it seemed we were right out in the Pacific Ocean, with the ship moving faster. We could hear the noise of the waves being parted by the bow. Japanese submarines lurked in this vicinity; we half-expected the loud bang of a torpedo at any moment. I thought how pleasant it would be to be knocked out with a single hit, all troubles instantly vanishing.

Not having a single companion I could really open my mind to, I just lay on the mattress. I had no spirit to do anything, and did not even want to move. As I lay motionless, putrid greenish pus kept oozing from my ears. I plugged them with tightly rolled paper but it was no use; in next to no time it had soaked through. I constantly renewed the paper but there was no limit to the flow. One of the other men suggested that I have my ears checked by the enemy medical officer, but I could not bring myself to do it. I had a faint hope that the infection might somehow lead to my being able to die. Indeed that was the only thing I could have hoped for. The idea that my ears might heal was a source of despair.

I had heard that in bygone days men had died by biting off their own tongues. At junior high school in our study of classical Chinese we had learnt the old story about Po-Yi and Shu-Ch'i, who I now thought of as kindred spirits. But I could not make myself go to such lengths. I considered myself despicable and tried to take myself to task, but all to no avail. A man cannot simply put an end to his life like an animal.

The problem lay in something more than just the means of death. So the problem was put off from day to day.

At times I would recall that dark battle at sea. When that shell had hit, somewhere at the rear of the bridge, nearly everyone present had been felled in an instant. The lookout man, the torpedo firing control men, and the helmsman standing near me, had all been killed. Why had I alone been miraculously spared? However much I pondered the outcome, I couldn't understand it. The only explanation was that I had been sheltered from the shell blast by being just behind the torpedo officer's assistant. He had been sacrificed in my stead, I supposed. He and I had not been standing in our normal positions when the shell hit. Just the very slight difference of one centimetre in distance, or of one second in time, and I might have been the casualty. When the ship sank and we were sucked under, though the captain and the navigating officer died, I alone floated up again.

Until then I had not been inclined to believe in 'destiny'. I now realised that there seemed to be an irresistible force at work in the world that cannot be countermanded by any human strength. Why had I not met death at that moment? How much better it would have been to have instantly ended it all—before one could even gasp—with no pain in dying. I envied the others their deathly departure.

As I lay on my side on the mattress, life and death continued to circle round endlessly in my thoughts. My faint expectations that something would turn up in the future made me postpone any possible solution.

We had been at sea for about three days; every day calm and clear. At last the ship arrived at some unknown destination.

Soon they brought us out of the hold onto the upper deck. Curious, we surveyed our surroundings. It was a tropical island; there was land on either side and the ship had dropped anchor in the narrow channel between. On both shores coconut palms grew luxuriantly. One side was low ground, while the other rose in hills from the shore towards dense jungle. We noticed two twin-engined Catalina patrol flying boats moored at the water's edge, as well as one freighter and several small craft at anchor.

In the evening we went ashore over a roughly built wharf. Black-skinned local inhabitants mingled with the American troops. I imagined that we were in New Caledonia but, from later inferences, I believe it must have been the New Hebrides.

The Americans forced us onto a small truck and we were driven along a rough road into forested hills. We soon arrived at what looked like a POW camp. By then dusk had fallen and we immediately lay down to sleep.

The next morning we studied our surroundings again. The camp covered an area about 100 square metres set out in a rectangle, well surrounded by a double barbed wire fence. Inside was a fairly large U-shaped shelter, simply constructed and covered by a roof thatched with palm fronds. In one wing camp beds with mosquito nets were set out, sufficient for our number. Comparing this with the enclosure at Guadalcanal, it was clear that this place had been purpose-built to accommodate POWs.

It was set in a coconut plantation and well back among the surrounding hills. It had no effective view so it was impossible to grasp the lie of the land. Occasionally we glimpsed cows grazing next to the fences.

Each morning a mild mannered, somewhat elderly, sergeant would come on his rounds of inspection.

The hot tropical weather continued each day. Thankfully, there was no particular work to be done as I was physically exhausted and spent most of the time stretched on my bed with nothing to think about except my inner struggle.

We soon discovered this new camp was no more than a staging post and that other Japanese prisoners had been here before us. Who were they? And what had become of them? We now felt a certain sense of camaraderie with those who had suffered the same fate. We sensed that we would not be here for long and our premonition proved correct.

About four or five days later a large transport ship awaited us off shore. Again we had no idea of our destination. Only one thing concerned me; wherever we went, I had to die.

They ordered four or five of us into an unbearably stuffy cabin in which I struggled to breathe. After some time we were transferred to a slightly more spacious cabin where breath came easier.

My ears still discharged pus and reacted with the warmth of the cabin to fuddle my brain and make me feel faint. But there was nothing so welcome as dying from cerebral anaemia or anything similar. I did take a bad turn and start to topple once, but without the longed for result. There was to be no easy death. In trepidation I stood before the cabin mirror to see what sort of face I presented. Having not seen my reflection since

Akatsuki sunk, I could hardly bear to look at the bedraggled, pallid, worn out spectacle that peered back at me.

On the ship we were given a compulsory shower—our first body wash for days.

A little later they called us out of the cabin one by one. Those previously gone did not return. Interrogation seemed the logical explanation, and when at last my turn came round this proved to be true. My interrogator was an officer attached to the Marines who knew Japanese fairly well. I learnt that he had spent some years in the Kansai district. What I told him about my name and rank was all nonsense, and at times I just said nothing. He was not very persistent so I managed to conceal the fact that I was an officer, pretending to be a seaman to frustrate their efforts.

4

New Caledonia

The calm voyage continued a few days longer, then, once more, our ship arrived at an unknown country. We emerged from our cramped cabin into a wide blue sky. Gently sloping hills spread in front of us, their slopes earthen-brown in the absence of trees. A little later we noticed two or three silver barrage balloons standing out in the cloudless sky. Their presence conveyed the importance of the island base.

A speedy landing craft delivered us ashore where we climbed onto a large truck which took off through the town. It had a quiet colonial air; few people ventured into streets drenched by the strong afternoon sun. Here and there the Stars and Stripes fluttered.

Soon we left the town behind, travelling along a narrow road flanked by an estuary on the left and hills on the right. At length we came to a division in the road. On the right sat a row of warehouse-type buildings sheathed with galvanised iron. The truck drove up to them and stopped to let us out.

It was a prefabricated building, simply constructed from a steel framework, and divided by a partition down the middle into front and rear compartments containing rows of camp beds. There were no windows and the building was dark and damp.

I had no spirit to do anything and simply lay on my bed. Nothing indicated that we would be moved for some time yet. At least during transportation my changing surroundings had provided a diversion and

I hadn't felt so troubled. But now that we had settled down, the battle of the spirit—that bitter internal struggle—surged back again.

It is essential to understand the Japanese concept of 'spirit'. It was a major reason why the war in the South Pacific became essentially a war of annihilation. Indoctrination started early. Educators, following government guidance, taught Japanese youth that they belonged to a special race, culturally and morally superior to the decadent and materialistic West. Officers and nationalistic educators passed on their contempt for American and European soldiers to recruits. Japanese military failures, such as the Battle of Midway, were closely kept secrets.

The notion of spirit also included the belief that the human will could surmount physical circumstance. Japanese officers taught their men, and believed themselves, that they could do things no other army could, simply because Japanese troops would not be denied. Much of Japanese education and military indoctrination dealt with mythological renderings of great acts of heroism which had one thing in common: the hero died in battle. Death in battle was portrayed as an honour to the family and a transcendent act on the part of the individual.

Every soldier carried a copy of the Emperor Meiji's Imperial Rescript of 1882. It contains a striking image. The cherry blossom, beloved of the Japanese, falls to earth in perfect form. The Rescript counsels, 'If someone should enquire of you concerning the spirit of the Japanese, point to the wild cherry blossom shining in the sun.' Thus the Japanese honoured the sanctity of the death of the young in battle.

I made every effort to judge where this new place was and concluded that it must be New Zealand. But after conversation with Japanese POWs in the neighbouring compartment, I realised that we were in the French colony of New Caledonia.

A good many days had passed since capture, and each of us had become accustomed to life as a POW. Not that every individual was notably or subjectively conscious of this; it just crept up on us. Watching many of the men going about things briskly, with no great conflict, I felt somewhat envious of them and believed that I alone was growing weaker. But, as time passed, a gradual change also came over my own inner soul; an ever-increasing desire for life gripped me. This was something new and a total surprise to me. I felt as though I had discovered an insidious traitor within my own self. Confrontation became more conscious and violent in my mind.

Until now I had not eaten much, being solely absorbed in my thoughts about dying. I maintained a blind self-confidence in the strength of my will. Increasingly, my instinct for life became a significant force. It sat in the centre of my being and tenaciously resisted ejection. Sometimes I found myself embracing life and was outraged by my conscience's betrayal. Such was the complex of anxieties which now surfaced.

Faced with this, a sense of urgency beat within me. If only I could have got my hand on a pistol, how simple it would have been. I thought about pouncing on one of the guards, or hanging myself—all sorts of things—but none seemed feasible. I allowed myself the luxury of not behaving like a lunatic.

I decided to completely abstain from food. There may have been various reasons why I'd failed in that conviction before, but now I was resolute.

A new struggle began and I grew weaker. Yet this was an indescribably bitter battle. Striving to be loyal to the call of conscience, my willpower grappled endlessly with my animal and bodily instincts. Which would be the stronger? How much more pleasant to have been killed by a single effort, but this was a drawn-out struggle of endurance.

Nearly all day I lay motionless on my cot assailed by violent pangs of hunger and thirst. Initially I ignored them with relative ease, but then they mounted a steady attack. My willpower struggled to keep things in check. One of our men brought me a cup of cocoa and placed it by the cot. Eventually, without thinking, I drank a mouthful. Only one mouthful, but it greatly settled my nerves. Before long the previous hunger and thirst came back on attack, stronger than ever.

If only I could drop off to sleep forever, just like this, I thought, as night came on. How I wish my eyes would never open again tomorrow, I prayed from my heart. Morning came round again and I opened my eyes. Must I fight anew with my conscience all day? Days dawned and days faded in the same way.

I wasted away. I had spent so much time lying down that the few times I had to go to the latrine I could hardly walk. Perhaps one more day, perhaps another...

To someone viewing this calmly and objectively, it would seem a pointless folly, but I struggled with my conscience in deadly earnest.

Then one day a motor vehicle stopped by the entrance and several American soldiers came in. Something seemed to be happening. Wasn't it one of our men leading them to me? An army captain led the group.

He squatted beside me, quickly inspected my ears, and without warning ordered his men to put me on a stretcher. Someone must have told the enemy soldiers about my condition. I felt a surge of anger that my motives had been misunderstood. I wanted to shout at them, but it would have been pointless.

They put me in an ambulance marked with a large red cross and sped back to town. In no time the vehicle stopped and they carried me into a building.

Inside were two rows of beds, totalling 12 or 13, with an aisle down the middle. I was surprised to see several Japanese POWs already there.

I gradually absorbed the nature of my surroundings. It was a detached building for POWs; hospital in name but not in appearance. It took me some time to get used to it.

My ears were treated and my wounds dressed. So much for ending my life! Surrounded by medical officers, nurses and medical orderlies, I lost my determination to die. I knew it was wrong, but I resolved to simply let things pan out. This attitude of self-abandonment gradually worked on my mind.

Under simple daily treatment from the medical officer, the wounds in my ears healed with surprising speed, bringing clarity to my hitherto befuddled state.

Each morning several army medical officers made their rounds, kindly examining us individually. Our hospital perched on a slope and, immediately above our ward separated by only a narrow alleyway, was a long two-storey building containing the American patients. The army doctors came to see us after completing their rounds in the main wards. They were humane gentlemen, considerate in their attitude towards us. Nonetheless, we continued to treat them as our enemy and were unable to meekly accept their kindness; it was unpleasant even to speak to them, so we always stayed silent.

One mealtime, when for some reason I was not eating much, a medical officer of dignified bearing noticed my lack of appetite and brought me a navel orange. It was embarrassing to be treated like this. To have an enemy go out of his way to be specially kind had a painful significance. But he appeared to have no underhand motives at all; it was just his usual behaviour. He took out a knife, and simply cut the fruit and offered it to me. He's got me beaten, I thought. In the face of love which had transcended very real national boundaries, I was overcome by a feeling of total defeat.

A few days after my arrival at the hospital, a group of soldiers again came with a stretcher. They carried me to the X-ray room in a separate ward and took several X-rays.

The next day a medical officer showed me one of them, and by words and gestures asked if it would be all right to operate. The X-ray revealed something square, like a shell fragment, in my right cheek. He seemed to be saying that they wanted to remove it. It was extremely polite of him to seek my consent, so as not to arouse misgivings on my part. I just nodded my head. Do what you like, I thought.

The operation was straightforward, but I felt dreadful that they had been so kind and polite over such a trifle. That such goodwill should be misinterpreted as malice could be looked at in different ways. But in actual fact, didn't their goodwill spring from their humanitarian views?

Japanese POWs must have seemed rare creatures to them; many American soldiers used to visit our ward for sightseeing. Among these were one or two who came to poke fun. Some said, "Hirohito, Tojo-Hang!" miming verdicts of hanging after the war had ended. While perhaps 'Tojo' could be tolerated, the bare untitled naming of 'Hirohito' jolted our sensibilities.

One day a nurse distributed cardboard boxes to each of us. These were Christmas presents from the Australian Red Cross Society, containing such things as tobacco and candy, and needles and thread. Previously I'd had absolutely no connection with Christianity, and this was my first experience of 'Christmas'. It was 24 December, Christmas Eve, 1942. As night came on a merry chorus of voices emerged from the upper building. I had no idea what they were singing, but I felt it was rather too boisterous for wartime.

For Christmas dinner we were treated to turkey. The lively celebrations continued in the other building; voices sung on endlessly. Soldiers who seemed to have had a few drinks wandered through our ward, then departed.

Then the night deepened, with all fast asleep, not a sound to be heard, everything locked in darkness. A single electric bulb shone dully in the ward. Only the MP and the medical orderly remained on duty. As I lay there my mind was fully alert, my eyes riveted on the pistol at the waist of the MP sitting nearby. If only I could get that into my hand, I kept thinking. But how futile; my opponent was a heavily built giant while I was a weak, tottering man. I lived on, miserable, as the Christmas night wore away.

Four or five days later my injuries had healed, and the time came for my discharge. In all I'd been there over two weeks, with the last few days spent exercising my legs. Having been in bed continuously, I couldn't walk unaided. I changed back from the neat patients' attire into my filthy clothing stained with dust and sweat. The army boots weighed heavy on my skinny legs. An enlisted man was discharged at the same time.

A sailor in a pure white summer uniform came to escort us. He wore an armband with the large dark blue letters NP sewn on a yellow background. He was little more than a youth and must have thought he was escorting two dreadful criminals. At the ward exit he chained us together in solid, metallic handcuffs, firmly fastened around our wrists. This seemed excessive treatment for weaklings who would have fallen over at the slightest push. We walked off, shuffling on unsteady feet, and when we came to steps our legs threatened to give way.

This was the first time in my life I'd had anything like handcuffs clapped on me, and the sensation was far from pleasant. To the ordinary man, anyone dragged along in shackles implies the greatest humiliation imaginable. Such a pitiful sight would repel most people. I felt dreadfully embarrassed to be seen, although I didn't know the people at all. Furthermore, that was the first time my weakness had been so completely exposed. Suppose they just abandoned us like that? We wouldn't have been able to do anything. Our absolute lack of freedom shocked me. However much we struggled, we would not be able to do a thing except wait to die.

Recalling this experience later, I was able to view the episode with thankfulness. In that moment I believe I gained contact with the true image of man. I had experienced every kind of degradation, humiliation, weakness, and bondage humankind can suffer. It is no small thing for a man to learn the limits of his own self, and for the first time my eyes were opened to feel deep sympathy for those who live in the same dark depths.

We returned again in the ambulance to the same warehouse-like building, where a young second lieutenant came out to take charge of us. He explained to me, very considerately, that the other men from *Akatsuki* had been sent on to New Zealand while I had been in hospital, and that I too would be sent there soon.

As I recall, not a single one of the *Akatsuki* men remained; their places had been taken by a completely new lot of about 20 Japanese POWs captured in a later battle off Guadalcanal. They also came from the crew of a destroyer, the *Takanami*. I could not bring myself to associate with their group and spent most of the following days lying alone on my cot, not wishing to interact with anyone.

On the eve of 1943, they suddenly transferred us. I thought we were off to New Zealand at last, but it proved not to be. Instead, they shifted us to a new prison camp, set well back in the hilly country beyond the first one.

We reached the new camp by grinding uphill along a motor road. It sat on the gentle slope of a little hollow. The camp spread out in an elongated rectangle, surrounded by barbed wire fences, and was subdivided into four compounds. The only entrance was in the short side at one end of the rectangle.

There was already one Japanese officer there in the compound furthest from the entrance. This was the first time I had come across an officer POW, and I felt in him a companion in adversity. He looked young, and apparently was an officer from the air service. But his face was unfamiliar and we never exchanged any words. He used to play cards by himself; he drew pictures or practised playing the harmonica, and seemed quite composed.

Towards the entrance was the compound in which we destroyer people were kept. In the middle stood five American army tents, and four or five of us were put into each of them. Here too things were as boring as ever, and I spent most of my time lying on my cot, lost in thought. At times the boredom was the hardest thing to take.

In the next compound there were about ten enlisted men, all air service personnel. When Tulagi in the Solomon Islands had been captured, at the same time as the airfield on Guadalcanal, some of them had escaped in a boat. After great effort they got as far as New Georgia, halfway back to friendly forces at our Shortland Islands base. There they had the misfortune to be seized by the natives and tied up for a lengthy period. Their hands were distorted and numbed by the bindings, and their skin and fingers turned purplish. It was a pitiful sight. It seemed the imprints would never fade.

My mental state underwent a further degree of change and my 'Just let things happen as they will' attitude became dominant. Whatever circumstances a person may be in, their desire for survival retains its power. Dostoevsky's words in *Notes from the House of the Dead* seem fully appropriate to this time: 'Yes, what a power of life there is in a man!

A man is a creature able to adapt himself to anything, and that is, I think, the best definition of him.' Truly profound words. Whatever dark depths of human existence a man may be reduced to, these words point to the first spark of revival. Having been through a life in captivity, the truth of these words has sunk deep into my very being. This most fundamental fact of humanity is no longer associated in my mind with shame or misery, but rather as something of greatest value to humankind—a source of true joy. The days continued to slip past.

When anyone is confronted with the reality of death, when they have no way of knowing whether they will be alive tomorrow, they live very much for the moment, instinctively and impulsively. Thus some people forget both shame and honour, and are carried away by the tendency to seek only the fulfilment of their urges. This tendency is extreme in those lacking self-control.

None of us ever had enough cigarettes. The Americans used to dole out five each per day, but these were insufficient. So some men would cut a cigarette in two and smoke each half separately. Then, horrible as it was, some would gather up discarded butts, roll them up again, and smoke them. That men could so calmly debase themselves indicated to me a lack of self-understanding, or simpleness of mind. Many of the men would also wait for an opportunity to beg shamelessly for cigarettes from the American guards. We had already been humiliated by being taken prisoner; to add to this shame by behaving like this was disgraceful. After all, had they forgotten their position as Japanese? How despicable. I yearned to shout my disapproval.

At other times a mischievous American soldier would fill an empty cigarette packet with small stones, and throw it over the fence to us. One of our men would immediately pounce on it, like a monkey in a cage swooping on food—a spectacle worthy of a zoo. Men reduced to such actions deserved the utmost pity.

But something else niggled. How would my attitudes stand up to questioning? I paused to reflect, and it struck me that there was really no difference in my craving for tobacco, it was merely that I had not turned my desire into action. My reason, intellect, sense of shame, and common sense just managed to keep my longings under control. When all is said and done, I was no different from the others. Theirs was a true reflection of humankind. Having reached this conclusion, I couldn't censure or blame them.

In my life in the navy, the idea of rank and status, and distinguishing people in terms of superior and inferior, had become well established in my psyche. Before long I even deluded myself that the basic human qualities between officers and men differed. But after facing the problems of captivity, 'rank' and 'position' seemed mere shadows. All humans, without exception, are in essence the same; there is no difference between an admiral or general and an ordinary seaman or private soldier.

Furthermore, my experiences taught me that on life's last stage, human reason and intellect are powerless. Our evaluation of human instinct leads us astray, perhaps being too simple-minded and optimistic. Indeed all sorts of human tragedies may have arisen from these errors of judgement.

The days dragged past in boredom. I resigned myself to being a POW and tried to defy the monotony by playing solo card games.

One day a kindly medical orderly shaved our faces with a safety razor. As it was more than a month and a half since we had shaved, our beards had grown considerably and our faces must have been filthy. It felt strange to have a smooth face.

The Americans interrogated us again. The man questioning me was the same captain who had questioned us on the ship. I strung some lies together and tried to say as little as possible until the time was up.

So the days passed, and at last departure for New Zealand arrived. The officer in charge of the POW camp, a young second lieutenant graduate of West Point Military Academy, unintentionally annoyed us with his Japanese vocabulary; he knew just two words: geisha and rickshaw. To make matters worse, someone felt obliged to indignantly answer him back that even in Japan there were a lot of things like motorcars.

They packed us into a large truck and we left the hills. Over in the hollows, barrage balloons crouched on the ground like enormous rabbits. The number of balloons flying over the town had increased during our captivity, obvious evidence that a full-scale defence installation was being set up on the island. It also seemed that the number of American troops had increased. Before long we stood on the wharf, gazing across the sea.

As we stared over the bay we saw, among other vessels, two large transport ships at anchor. They were luxury-liners, painted over in wartime grey. The weather was fine but the wind gusted and the waves ran high. In the background Noumea, capital of the French colony, spread out on the slopes of the gentle hills, facing the sea.

They loaded us into a landing craft and, buffeted by the waves, we bumped out to one of the transports.

Once aboard, we were put in two cabins on the starboard side of the upper deck. The porthole was shut, and the interior dim. There were nine bunks arranged in three tiers, but we were not too cramped.

As the vessel made its way south, I kept to myself. Others played cards, or engaged in small talk. Now and then the guard would open the porthole to allow fresh air into the cabin, but all I saw was the boundless expanse of ocean.

What sort of place was New Zealand? What would be waiting for us? Certainly we were all interested to find out. At the Naval Academy I had read an article about the Naval Training Squadron's visit to New Zealand, but my knowledge of the country ended there. The capital was Wellington, the largest city was Auckland, there were hot springs at Rotorua, and the native inhabitants were the Maori; as for the rest...

5

New Zealand

Some days later when they opened our porthole, we saw a shoreline within hailing distance, steep cliffs stretching both ways. The land and the sea sparkled under the sunlight like a postcard picture, and I tingled with the peculiar excitement experienced by sea-going men when they see a new country for the first time.

As we neared the harbour entrance the porthole was closed, and the cabin was shut off again from the outside world. Inside, I strained my ears to hear the surrounding noises, and tried to judge the progress of the ship's entry into port.

Soon they ordered us to move. We filed out of the dark cabin and lined up in the passageway. By the time we were led out in single file on the other side, the ship was tied up alongside the wharf.

Several small trucks awaited us. As we got to the bottom of the gangway we were loaded into them and quickly driven away. As the trucks had canopies, we only glimpsed what was outside through the cracks, but we obviously ran along a main paved city street.

A short distance from the wharf, the truck entered a gate facing the main road. Inside, there was a building very much like a prison. That night we were locked up in pairs in a room the size of four and a half *tatami* mats (2 m by 4 m). A number of similar rooms, apparently single cells, formed rows along either side. A little window covered with a grating sat high in the wall and the door had a tiny round aperture for a warder to peer through. There were no beds at all. I was given one blanket and had no choice but to wrap it around me and lie on the wooden floor. Now well south of the tropics, I was still thin and weak and the cold night was hard. I felt sorry for myself.

The next morning, the American forces unexpectedly treated us to the kind of splendid breakfast that they usually had. Afterwards we gathered in an internal courtyard where soldiers wearing different uniforms waited for us; these were our New Zealand escorts, and this was our first contact with them. They did not look like regular fighting men. Instead they looked like time-expired soldiers or hired auxiliary troops.

The truck we rode in spent some time winding through the city streets, eventually arriving at the railway station. The signs announced the name of the city: Auckland. I caught sight of buildings taller than any in Japan. The city and its culture exuded a British atmosphere.

We travelled in a special carriage attached to the end of a normal passenger train. To someone fresh from fighting, everything seemed somehow settled; the soldiers escorting us were relaxed and everything seemed free from the direct touch of the fires of war.

Soon after the train started, the soldiers ordered the window blinds opened. The sun's light flooded immediately into the narrow carriage and the scenery of this beautiful, strange land began to unfold before us. Intense relief flooded through me, as though everything had been liberated from darkness.

Behind us Auckland City spread out in colourful beauty, a stark contrast to the blackness of the cities of Japan. In places the railway line passed close to the sea, where many yachts floated on gentle waves. The sea seemed well loved. It was January—high summer and the sky was clear and bright.

But my disgrace was never far away and always tempered any sense of enjoyment. The road before me led only to death. After all, for a 'living corpse' none of life's pleasures are to be enjoyed; everything loses colour and becomes meaningless.

The train stopped at various stations along the way and we saw civilians getting on and off. Further into the countryside human habitation became sparse. From about evening onwards, the train threaded through hill country, crawling up and down steep gradients. On both sides the pastureland continued. One of the other prisoners, assessing the lonely landscape, surmised that we were being transported to hard labour in mountain coalmines. Because he was so terribly serious about it, it all seemed rather ludicrous. It seemed a bizarre comedy and I was almost overcome by an urge to laugh.

By now complete darkness enveloped everything; the carriage windows ahead contained the only light as the train wound round the curves.

The good soldiers of the escort had settled down and one group seemed to be playing cards in the corner. We were all tired, voices became infrequent, and the carriage occupants slumbered. Although I wanted to sleep, it wouldn't come. I spent the night dozing lightly.

Early the next morning the train pulled into some town where the carriages were shunted before the train moved off again. Apparently we were on a branch line, as most of the carriages had been left behind. The kind of pastureland that I had only seen in photographs now unrolled before my eyes. It was like a dream—the fenced paddocks with flocks of sheep, forest here and there; houses set sparsely on the landscape; flowing rivers. The train then passed through splendid rolling country dotted with fleecy sheep. Now and then we saw herds of cattle grazing on the paddocks. It was all so broad, composed, and serene—a scene of tranquillity that said, "Where is the war that you were mixed up in?" The weather was fine and warm. My mood relaxed again, and I almost forgot about being a POW. I thought in that moment if I could spend my whole life in a place like this, how happy I would be. A new world opened fresh and large in my imagination.

The train arrived at our destination at around 3 p.m. a small country town called 'Featherston'. It was situated near the capital city and my first impression on alighting was of a town far smaller and more deserted than I had ever imagined. We stepped off the train and they gathered us into two army trucks.

When the trucks left behind the quiet rows of houses, pastureland spread out again, with a single straight road running through it. On our right was a tall shelterbelt of trees. After a short ride, an English signboard indicated the location of the POW camp. Here we swung left and entered an enclosure surrounded by tall barbed wire fences. The compound sat in the middle of a stark unbroken plain. Disappointed, I muttered, "What on earth! What's this?"

Apart from a few simple barrack-like structures, there was no 'building' worthy of the name. A crowd of men in strange black hats and black clothing milled around within the enclosure. As I looked more carefully, I realised that they were Japanese POWs. Initially I was amazed that there were so many. Mingled with the pleasure of joining other captives was the nagging sense of humiliation at having to face them.

We newcomers were set apart in a separate small wire-fenced compound. A road ran north and south down the middle of the prison camp. Our area was on the eastern side, while across the road were two large wire-fenced compounds in which the first Japanese POWs were held. At last, we felt like we had reached our destination and no more journeying was likely. Nevertheless, as a final destination it was a more meagre sort of place than I had hoped for.

Everyone lived in tents. Even shabby huts would have been better. I soon learnt that the POW camp was still under construction; civilian workers came in and the work progressed. Subsequently we POWs had to make up several shifts to help out.

First they issued us with clothing and eating utensils. These were extremely plain, immediately indicating the difference between the American way and this British way of doing things. The atmosphere was completely down-to-earth, simple and rustic.

Next, army doctors put us through a medical inspection, and our personal details were recorded.

One of their interpreters made a particular impact on us. He would visit and spare no effort over the smallest things on our behalf. His name was Robertson, with a rank corresponding to a Japanese Army warrant officer. He was a bespectacled, gentle person, kind in every way, and in general lacked the usual characteristics of a military man.

With nothing special to do all day, many of the men set about playing cards and gambling their cigarette ration.

After about ten days, we newcomers transferred from the small compound into the one immediately in front, which contained a large group of the original detainees. Here I was reunited with the men from *Akatsuki* and also confronted with the fraught atmosphere of the camp; the situation was far from calm.

The Japanese POWs held at Featherston at that time included some 200 men from the cruiser *Furutaka*, sunk in the Battle of Savo Island. Added to them were approximately 400 drafted workers from the Guadalcanal airfield construction units, captured by the Americans, and these formed the main strength. Other than that, there were also a few from other naval ships (including *Akatsuki*), and some from the air service and army. In all there would have been about 750 of us.

These were divided into two compounds, and in our compound *Furutaka* crew formed the main body. The drafted construction workers occupied the other compound. I heard that some of the *Furutaka* POWs had been taken to the American mainland. There were also about seven officers, living separately in a detached compound. Almost as an afterthought, one German POW was put away all alone. Later he disappeared from the prison camp, unnoticed by us.

When you have nearly 400 men living collectively in one compound, naturally some sort of control is necessary. But here our previous military orders and systems of subordination no longer had any binding powers. Each individual was able to behave arbitrarily and no one could say anything against it. There was no coherence within the body and no end to trouble. Nothing could be said against those who were well behaved, but a minority of violent men determined on a course of provocation.

We latecomers didn't know what had happened previously in the compound, but we felt the strained relationships between the officers and a minority of the petty officers. One section of the men planned to start a riot; the atmosphere was menacing, and seemed unlikely to calm down. For this reason, the officers responsible for contacts and negotiations with the New Zealanders were greatly troubled by what course to adopt.

The fixed points in each day's routine, apart from the three meals, were the morning and afternoon roll calls conducted by the duty officer, and the commandant's tour of inspection after 10 a.m. Other than these, only light duties had to be performed. Hand-made *shogi* (chess) and *go* (draughts) sets helped pass the time, as did gambling.

The camp commandant at that time was a lieutenant colonel; a lean figure, a man of few words and a chilly manner, a character completely in the stamp of an English gentleman.

Since Guadalcanal, I had concealed from the enemy the fact that I was an officer. However, after settling in our new surroundings, this caused mutual embarrassment between myself and the other men. When the others suggested it, I undertook procedures to be placed in the officers' compound. But I could not bring myself to reveal my correct rank or name and continued to be known as Masaharu Kawai, a junior lieutenant.

A strained and oppressive atmosphere hung heavy in the prison camp as each day dragged past. As communication between those in charge and the prisoners broke down, it seemed trouble would break out. It was like a mass of snow descending a steep slope, inexorably growing and accelerating as it progresses. Sure enough, the inevitable happened.

The prime point at issue was over the question of work by POWs. According to the 'World Prisoners-of-War Convention', officers are not required to work, while non-commissioned officers (or petty officers) and other ranks are obliged to. The New Zealanders, under cover of the rules of the POW Convention, formally imposed the obligation to work. In this, as far as they were concerned, their actions were perfectly appropriate, and they probably felt there was no inconsistency in their position. However, consider too the feelings of the Japanese, who were in no mood to work for an enemy country. To those trained in the Japanese armed forces, such a thing would go beyond all that was proper. Of course the work itself was not important, but it was the question of honour. It was an issue based on a difference between cultures and traditions, a point which the New Zealanders were completely unable to understand.

Some of the men urged resolute resistance; others advocated moderation and others thought only of sensibly going about their lives. In these conditions, with every man holding a conflicting opinion, it was as though someone had upset a hive of bees.

Before now the advocates of resolute resistance, a section among the petty officers and men had been planning to start a riot. The idea was that riots should be instigated and repeated until every one of us died. They urged this idea on the officers too, insisting that the plan should start immediately. As talk progressed, the men got very excited. They imputed neglect of duty to a section of the officers, whipping up feelings strong enough to incite murder between friends and comrades. It was a turbulent atmosphere, with the problem of work and the idea of a riot intertwined.

Initially I was able to sympathise with the ideas of the resolute resistance faction. Any number of times I had been swept by the impulse that we should start a riot and be able to die in it. However, when I thought this over critically, I wondered if it would not be more appropriate to go individually to death, without involving others who didn't hold our views. The resolute group decided that they were the real Japanese fighting men, while the others were weaklings and cowards. In their minds, the matter of death was not to be confronted individually, but was a group responsibility.

In opposition, the moderate faction insisted that we did not have to die and that, although obviously in a bad position, we had no choice but to live in accordance with the rules of the POW Convention. Neither view satisfied our feelings. The contradiction and confusion stemmed from the traditions that we held as members of the Japanese armed forces. Thus emotion ran ahead of calm consideration, rushing on towards a crisis, but with the mentality of those times it could hardly be avoided.

Amongst the officers, individual opinions differed so they were unable to express a single coherent opinion. This too caused concern. I was tormented by not holding any firm convictions of my own. On the question of work, we had no choice but to refuse it in principle. Considering the turns and shifts in negotiations with the other side, it looked like there might yet be a positive outcome. In any case, we considered it unlikely that the enemy would do anything rash.

But as things turned out, this conclusion proved simple-minded.

6

Riot

The day of reckoning came upon us sooner than expected. On the 25 February 1943, the prison camp authorities brought out an armed platoon, as though planning to solve the problem resolutely by forcing our side to make a clear choice whether or not to send out working parties as ordered.

That morning two officers from *Furutaka* (Lieutenant Nishimura and Junior Lieutenant Adachi) had gone to the enlisted men's compound in order to play a part in the negotiations, but before long one of them was marched back in an agitated state, grabbed under the arms by an enemy soldier on either side. Tension was rising in number two compound.

Time passed while we anxiously wondered what would happen, how it would turn out, when suddenly the sound of rifles cracked out with violent force.

I was stunned, but there was nothing I could do. The dreadful choking moments as shots rang out dragged past. End it all quickly was all I could think... I helplessly imagined what was going on in the other compound.

After a while the rifle fire ceased. Outside the compound, we could see the New Zealand soldiers bustling around. It was not easy for me to control my agitation.

Later that evening we learnt further details about the shooting from the enlisted men who delivered our meal. Approximately 240 prisoners, seated or squatting close together in a quadrangular area between recently completed huts, faced an armed guard of 47 men. They circled the prisoners, occupying positions at both ground level and on hut roofs. Amongst the guards tension mounted while some of the prisoners picked up stones. The camp adjutant, Lieutenant James Malcolm, insisted that Adachi come out from amongst the men. He refused, determined to stay with the sit-in. The Japanese maintained passive resistance and requested face-to-face dialogue with the camp commandant on the work party issue.

A warning shot was fired, stones were hurled, and the guards opened fire as the POWs rushed towards them. In less than a minute, 122 Japanese lay wounded or dead. One New Zealand guard died from wounds caused by a ricocheting bullet. Three other guards and the camp's duty officer of that day were hospitalised as a result of the shooting.

I reproached myself without limit, why wasn't I there with them? Shouldn't I myself have died there right in front of all the others? A mere creature of belated remorse and chaotic mind, I was deeply shocked. I was utterly crushed by my helplessness as a man.

But I was also profoundly indignant with the enemy. However much the Japanese POWs disobeyed orders, these were excessive measures against unarmed men. The commandant's cold face floated before me. As I thought of this deed, combined with the imperial traditions of Britain, I loathed and cursed them all.

> If only one's power be strong, what then is justice?
> It is well to use it;
> The means matter not.

These lines, read during my Naval Academy days, came to mind. The German Vice Admiral von Manthey had quoted them from Goethe's *Faust*, with reference to Britain, in his *Outline of the World History of Naval Warfare*.

But in retrospect, has not Japan been the same? Young then, I genuinely believed that Japan's battles were a holy war. But one great discovery gained as a POW was that your opponent has his own standpoint and version of justice. We believed our view was absolutely correct. Yet our certainty started to waver when we came out into the wide new world. Gradually our outlook opened up, from a view of things centred on Japan to a view of the world as a whole. I began to wonder where such things as true justice might be found. After all, whatever nice things you may say about humankind, is there, in the end, anything more than the mere drive to fulfil our own desires? Are not nations ultimately motivated by their own interests? Before long my mind had gone on to consider the faithlessness of man to man, and the malice of man to man, which go past national boundaries. This completely disenchanted me.

The shooting brought home painfully, to each individual, the limitations of being a POW. In the face of armed strength, human self-assertion is futile. We felt beaten with hammer blows to the head into accepting our fate. Nonetheless, the experience gave us a sense of identity to unite as one. That is what we heard from those who represented us at the respectful ceremonies in memory of those who had died.

But what happens to a man when he dies? My questions about humanity continued to deepen. The more I thought about it, the more I was tormented by a world full of contradictions. In one way I thought those who had died were better off. I was even envious. I was a POW and there was no joy in this life. Is it really happiness for a man to live, or wouldn't it be better to die? But where could I find a yardstick to measure this?

It must be admitted that we humans are a wayward lot, and not much can be done about it; possibly this is an inherent failing. The atmosphere inside the prison camp calmed, internal control was set up, and working parties went out. The passage of time gradually dimmed the violent memories.

As officers we had nothing to do but eat three meals a day—it was like being caged in a human zoo. With nothing to set our hands to, we spent our time just lighting and smoking roll-your-own tobacco, which was freely available. Now and then we would play *shogi*, but as we were all poor players it soon palled. I tried playing solitaire, but could stir up no interest; the inanity of it drove me to distraction. When I took the advice of others and set to learning *go*, until then unknown to me, I became quite crazy about it.

Now and then in the prison camp we had visitors from outside; we were treated as rarities. Before I arrived, the Labour Party Prime Minister, Mr Fraser, had visited. One day several smartly dressed American officers arrived. Among them was one who said that before the war he had been at Rikkyo University in Tokyo, and he seemed genuinely glad to meet us. Apparently he had been called up to serve as an interpreter.

During our monotonous POW life the thing we most wanted to know, and which constantly occupied our thoughts, was the war's progress. But hardly any news reached us; we were starved for information.

Now and then the most amazing rumours flew around. One day, for example, the news from the enlisted men's compound was that the Japanese Army had landed in Australia. While we felt slightly uneasy about Japan's future, our indoctrination of Japan being the immortal land of the gods meant that any idea of defeat was unthinkable.

The shooting occurred in February. Then March and April passed and autumn took hold. Each day pleasant, dry weather continued; perhaps our minds were responding to the serene monotones of surrounding nature.

The construction of the prison camp continued steadily. First the two compounds to take the enlisted men and the construction workers respectively were completed. Replacing the previous tent accommodation, rows of simple prefabricated huts were set out, each accommodating eight men; also mess halls, cookhouses and ablution blocks had been built. Inside every one was a two-level pair of wooden bunks. The huts so resembled enlarged dog kennels that they were nicknamed 'dog houses', in English.

After completion of these compounds, work continued on a hospital and a joinery factory. Last of all, our officers' compound was fitted into the construction program. Because of the work, we officers had to make one more temporary shift. This next place was in the north-west corner of the prison camp. For the time being, we lived on as before in tents while the enlisted men lived in new buildings.

About then a fresh group of 20 or 30 Japanese soldiers arrived, apparently from the Solomons. They were pitifully thin and looked wretched; we wondered whether we ourselves had been like that previously. Among them was an army officer, a junior lieutenant. They boosted our numbers to about 800. These new arrivals were the last until the final year of the war when ten arrived from Paita POW camp in New Caledonia.

One day the interpreter Robertson came specially to us with a sheet from an English language newspaper. There was a photograph of the Admiral Isoroku Yamamoto, Commander in Chief of the Combined Fleet, and a news item stating that he had been killed in the war. The newspaper treated this news in a minor way, placing it halfway down a column with no detailed explanation. What had happened? The ill omen sank us into gloom. What had happened, in fact, was that the plane carrying Commander in Chief Yamamoto had been ambushed above the island of

Bougainville and shot down by American fighter planes.

Before we knew it, autumn deepened and our first winter at Featherston approached, with each morning and evening growing a little colder. Although this was 40 degrees south, the cold was not severe considering the latitude. From what we heard, this country had autumn-like weather all year round, and during our following three years we seldom saw anything like snow.

A battered old drum stove had been discarded nearby. We set it up in the open air near the tent and together drew warmth from it. Around this single source of heat, we spent pleasant times engrossed in small talk. We watched the fire blaze, then die into embers... Every day without exception, we played *go* as our principal occupation, and forgot the passing of the hours. With seven men in a small double-layered tent, cut off from the outside air, we hardly felt the cold at night.

Once the enlisted men sent us a set of mah-jong tiles. Although I say mah-jong tiles, and they were competently made, they were wooden and far from matching the real thing. At first we all played together, but perhaps because it didn't suit my temperament, I couldn't get enthusiastic and would drop out partway through. In the enlisted men's and construction workers' compounds, mah-jong and gambling were at the height of popularity. These POWs believed they had no right to live and, lacking future prospects, inevitably fell into a lifestyle of momentary pleasure and decadence. It gave no pleasure to witness young men, who should be straightforward and honest, heading for moral corruption.

I too led such a life, but my conscience had not entirely gone to sleep. When I lay on my bed at night, enveloped in utter darkness and boundless space, my conscience came to life again. In daytime I was diverted by the world around me, and forced to face outwards. But when night came my thoughts naturally turned inwards and a persistent voice started to nag. I had no sense of stability in life. But in spite of this I could not degenerate utterly into a life of nihilism. "Oh, how I long for that one truth which will never let me go astray! If I could only discover it..." The emptiness of my daytime existence made my search for the truth blaze ever more strongly.

Then it happened. News that a missionary, who had previously been in Japan, would be coming to the camp as a military chaplain...

When I heard this I felt a sense of oppression. In this enemy country we felt caught in servile bondage; on top of that, would we have to endure our spiritual freedom being shackled by Christianity? My understanding of Christianity at that time was the same as the preconceptions held by most Japanese. We thought that it was some sort of butter-flavoured Euro–American religion, and that to believe in it meant spiritual capitulation to those cultures. Christianity was taken to be something of a sickly, poor-spirited, feminine religion. I resolved that, even if this missionary did come, I would have absolutely nothing to do with Christianity.

Eventually the missionary arrived on a visit, accompanied by the interpreter Captain Ashton. Captain Ashton was a scholarly type of Englishman, who for many years taught at schools in Japan, and was already fairly well on in life. Together with the interpreter Robertson he treated the Japanese POWs in the most well disposed manner.

The missionary introduced to us by Captain Ashton wore a suit. First impressions indicated a mild personality, with a somewhat florid face and hair relatively thin on top. He seemed to have forgotten most of his Japanese and didn't say much other than something about coming here as a military chaplain. Before long he took his leave. Nonetheless, my mind hardened; no blue-eyed, redheaded foreign missionary would be allowed to tie down my thoughts. I thought missionaries were no more than spies or magicians, so I built a fence around my mind.

7

The Officers' Compound

Around about June 1943 our new compound was completed and we shifted in.

The prison camp site formed a near rectangle, with its sides facing more or less directly north, south, east and west. The whole circumference, a considerable area, was ringed by barbed wire. The interior was further subdivided into various compounds by tall barbed wire fences, with the new officers' compound in the south-eastern part of the camp.

Immediately to the north was a drill ground for the New Zealand troops stationed at the prison camp. It was at least twice the size of our compound, about as big as a rugby field.

Next, adjoining us immediately to the west, were the hospital facilities. These newly constructed buildings were permanent and we heard they intended to continue using the site for a hospital after the war. Enclosed to the east and south by the drill ground and hospital respectively, two separate compounds had been set up for the enlisted men and the construction workers. To the west, across a wide road which ran north and south through the camp, there was a large area with workshop buildings.

The town of Featherston lay due west of the prison camp and just beyond it were mountains, a hilly range stretching away to the north, limiting the view. The railway ran along the foot of the mountains. Only a few trains went past each day—when the faint sound of their steam whistles called, they evoked vague thoughts of home.

In addition to these installations there was also a long narrow strip of land, stretching east and west along the southern side, containing the enemy establishments. Immediately to the south of our officers compound was the motor vehicle pool, and beyond that a public highway. Not many people went past each day, and motor vehicles only occasionally, but it was our only point of contact with the outside world. Beyond the highway stretched civilian grassland farms and tree plantations. Further in the distance we glimpsed what looked like the high mountains of the South Island.

Over the eastern boundary spread wide pastures, with only a single fence between us. Flocks of sheep and herds of cattle grazed there and the sheep eventually became our best friends. Far away at the eastern limit of a broad pasture, a shelterbelt of trees ran north and south, and to the left was what we took to be the farmer's house. Apart from the hilly range stretching from the west to the north, the topography was pretty much a broad plain.

Our officers' compound was about 100 metres square, surrounded by a double barbed wire fence with the sole entrance at the western end of the southern side. Immediately on the right was a 'doghouse' used by the cook and batman, grouped with a combined cookhouse-food store, and a dining room—three buildings in all.

Next to the neighbouring hospital were five doghouses in two rows, constituting another group. In each were two wooden beds. A recreation room had been erected by the northern fence. This was the largest building in the compound; its inside was bare and bleak with only three stoves, placed for heating in winter. A little to the east of this recreation room was a combined bathhouse-latrine. These buildings were all of simple barrack-like construction, uniformly dark green; they were all set generally towards the western end, leaving the eastern end with plenty of empty ground which we later used as a vegetable garden.

The new environment brought us a new mood. We had shifted so many times that we had never felt settled, but here we made ourselves a little more at home. Of course each of us was concerned with how long the war would last, but we couldn't imagine a quick end.

After the shooting incident, the commandant was replaced by another for a while. He was a major much older than the soldiers. In contrast to his predecessor, he had a frank and warm personality and was easy to get to know. During the First World War he had served with the famous 'Anzacs' (Australia–New Zealand Army Corps) and had taken part in the European war. He once told us how in those days on a voyage to Europe the transport ships had been escorted in the Indian Ocean by a destroyer from the Japanese Navy. He remarked with some feeling how, in an ironic reversal of fate, the friend of yesterday had become the enemy of today. It seemed he could not forget the heartening sense of security, difficult to put in words, of that time when we had been allies.

"War no good!" he would say light-heartedly in English, his tone conveying a deep grain of truth based on experience.

Day after day was boring beyond all measure, too many hours and nothing to do with them. So some, myself included, dozed on our beds and daydreamed. When pleasant thoughts would not drift our way, we indulged in small talk, or played *go* and *shogi*. Eventually a ping-pong table and equipment made the recreation room less bleak. But before long we tired of that too. Those of us interested in agriculture looked forward to the coming of spring, when the large vacant stretch of ground could be cultivated. Perseverance prevailed.

Ensconced in the new compound, we managed to get our hands on the New Zealand daily newspapers. Ostensibly, POWs were not permitted to read newspapers, but they came in by a back-door route. The working parties of enlisted men used to come to our compound on routine duties and secretly bring us newspapers. Starved of news, at last we managed to get a glimpse of the current world situation.

As a member of the British Commonwealth, most of New Zealand's troops were stationed in the northern hemisphere so European war news was treated more prominently than that in the Pacific arena. Their concerns seemed to be centred on their British mother country. In July and August 1943 the Mediterranean campaign for the liberation of the island of Sicily held sway. Such articles made me realise how mistaken my views had been, i.e. that Japan was the centre of everything. The insight of being able to understand our opponents' viewpoint was learnt while held amongst them. Our unique third-party standpoint as POWs opened me up to a new world outlook.

No great change was yet developing in the Pacific war but, by degrees, the strategic balance shifted. Already Guadalcanal had been lost. During the three-night sea battle, when my destroyer was sunk, several hundred Americans were killed. Four American destroyers—*Barton, Monssen,*

Cushing and *Laffey*—were sunk. The *Atlanta* was burnt out and later scuttled while its sister ship *Juneau* was sunk by a submarine torpedo while retiring from battle. We lost the destroyers *Akatsuki* and *Yudachi*. Our flagship *Hiei* was so badly damaged that it had to be scuttled, with survivors taken off by other Japanese ships. On the third night the *Washington* approached unseen and wrecked the *Kirishima* with a few minutes of radar-controlled fire from its nine 16 inch guns.

In the Solomon Islands, from July through to August, the enemy had secured successive footholds, like stepping stones, on the central islands of Rendova, New Georgia, and Vella Lavella. Over in eastern New Guinea, MacArthur's forces were gradually pushing forward along the coastline. A brief newspaper paragraph had reported in May that American forces had recaptured Attu Island in the Aleutians. Daily, brutal battles raged between the forces at sea and on Pacific islands. But we POWs lived out our now uneventful prison camp lives. Ringed by barbed wire palisades, altogether segregated from events outside, this little plot formed a separate world of its own.

Already more than half a year had passed since our arrival and our life, influenced by the idyllic natural environment, developed its own peculiarities. As time passed, those first moods after capture—of confusion, pending mental derangement, and demoralisation—were laid to rest. To all appearances we were now stable and mild men. The majority were governed by self-centred and utilitarian thoughts, whereby it seemed wisest to live only for the moment.

In the enlisted men's and construction workers' compounds, mah-jong gambling seemed to flourish as much as ever, but everyone eventually tires of always doing the same thing. This led to the novel outlet of making things like bamboo flutes and violins. The flutes were initially made from spare tent poles, and when those had gone we used wood. So tunes like *Harusame (Spring Rain)* and *Chidori no Kyoku (Songs of the Plover)* enlivened the still nights of that foreign land. A number of hand made violins were produced, and about then the enlisted men were supplied with genuine musical instruments.

Japanese are clever with their fingers, and various talented men made all sorts of wooden handicrafts. For example they made walking sticks, carved elephants (a favourite with the guards), and mah-jong tiles. They exchanged these with the guards for cigarettes, or for money with which they bought musical instruments and other luxuries.

Considering these activities, some POWs reflected that we should not continue to waste our lives like this, with no idea of how long our present state might continue. At last some began to realise the hollowness of a casual life lived only for the moment. One manifestation of this was the spreading study of English in the compounds, a feeling that you might as well improve language skills rather than squander time. This became something of a fashion, a utilitarian way of thinking based on personal gain, but it was better than spending the days aimlessly.

Around August, at the height of the southern hemisphere winter, the missionary we had been introduced to was permanently appointed as military chaplain to the whole POW camp. Each of the prisoners' compounds hosted a meeting once a week. The Padre's name was Troughton, and he had by now quit his suit for an army captain's uniform. Voices raised in hymns new to our ears wafted through the windows of the recreation room. At first the meetings attracted only four or five men, while most of us regarded them with scornful eyes. What's this? Prisoners listening to talk about Christianity from an enemy missionary... Although I didn't say that, I too regarded them critically.

8

'Sorrow in Victory'

POW life was governed by interminable monotony, as I have already described. This alone was bad enough but locked away in this little compound, completely isolated, one's brain gradually grew feebler. The occasional newspaper held little consolation.

If only there'd been some reading matter in Japanese, we would all have devoured it. Eventually they did get us several dozen books in Japanese, which helped relieve the boredom. These apparently belonged to the interpreter Robertson, who must have brought them back on his evacuation from Japan.

At first I treated the books with disdain. But when I began reading them, I found much pleasure. The titles extended to various subjects, Christianity amongst them, including many by Toyohiko Kagawa. I particularly remember *Shi-sen wo Koete* (*Face to Face with Death*) and *Seisho no Shakai Undo* (*Social Movements in the Bible*). There were several English translations of books by the same author, *A Grain of Wheat* and others. Also included were general literature, novels, and the like. Several pre-war magazines like *Bungei Shunju* (*Literary Annals*) and *Chuo Koron* (*Central Opinion*) brought back wistful memories.

It so happened that one of these volumes contained an article by Roka Tokutomi, which for some reason caught my eye. This article dated from shortly after the Russo–Japanese War. It was entitled 'Sorrow in Victory'.

This did not catch my interest when I first read it, but it must have left some impression. Later, after the third reading, it gradually took a stronger hold. As a POW, my eyes were opened for the first time to some of the serious problems of human life. The article provided a ray of light and raised new hope and courage within me. My views on humanity, the world and history, had collapsed. I was constantly tormented by thoughts about death, doubt and pain, while still seeking an answer.

The article's background was Roka's visit to Russia, and he took as his starting point the deep emotion he felt as he stood on the Sparrow Hills on the outskirts of Moscow. Here Napoleon had stood, after his invasion of Russia at the head of a vast army, and looked down at last on his objective, Moscow. Tolstoy put something about this in *War and Peace*.

Roka put it this way:

> Gentlemen! In the event, at this hour, this moment, what emotions must have stirred within him? I think he would certainly not have been shouting 'Hurrah!' He had led his Grand Army across the frontier of Russia, had won an uncertain victory at the Battle of Borodino, and would now enter Moscow. With this Moscow lying before his eyes, and his desired objective nearly attained, his heart should have been filled with gladness, and he should have leapt for joy. But I believe that, while Napoleon of course would not have been unhappy, would not some undefinable fleeting emotion have restrained his gladness? The moment he stood on the Sparrow Hills was truly the turning point of his history. With this instant as the dividing line, his enterprise went on to suffer a setback. That he extinguished this sense of sorrow, and went on forcibly to have his own way, led on and on to the piling up of errors, and right until he drew his last breath on St Helena he gained no understanding of the truth before he passed away for ever. Whether he would be considered the personification of Will, or whether he would end as a man of Truth, could only have been decided by this fleeting sense of sadness. Regrettably he extinguished it, and passed from this world...
>
> What is this sorrow in victory? It is the grief of one who yearns for the infinite, when he learns his limitations. It is the sorrow of one who wishes to have his own way and extend his own interests, when he aims to cross over to boundless shores beyond, but then realises there is a great impassable gulf between. Grief like this... at times attacks men's minds with irresistible force.

Roka put it beautifully. It came through to my soul with compelling force. It gently touched a source of grief somewhere deep in our hearts. Then he digressed, going on to say something about the outcome of the Russo–Japanese War.

...however much we may blame or punish that hated country Russia, it will never be enough. What could we achieve in the end even if we aroused the whole country and dedicated our whole selves to it? One gets vexed thinking of it. Just as defeat is sorrow, so an incomplete victory is sorrow also. Japan has felt this sorrow of an incomplete victory, and this sorrow felt by our nation is by no means unconscious. That Japan has been newly born and is growing, and newly developing and progressing, is wrapped up in this.

What then is prosperity for Japan? What is progress for Japan? Does it lie in increasing the army from 13 divisions to 17 divisions? Does it lie in increasing the navy from 200,000 tons to 300,000 tons? Oh no! Japan has not yet enough self-understanding in its own heart. This is where it ought to develop. This is what ought to progress.

In this way Roka indicated that the secret of new birth lay right there in this 'sorrow', and also that this must be a new birth of the mind.

...after all, men are saddened by limitations, and are driven to long for the infinite. Be it determination or be it emotion, these will be fulfilled, and when they pass away a void will be left and sorrow will be born. That is what we must grasp. Would you drive away the shadows and take hold of the truth? Would you get beyond the superficial and seek those eternal things within? Is the glory of the rose of Sharon to be admired for a morning, or should we seek first eternal life? This is truly the solemn question not to be put off for a moment.

We have only one aim in view, that the lifespan of individual people, whether there is any significance in it or not, should be extended endlessly or to 50 years or 100 years. But this should be decided by just what we are seeking, and by what aim we are progressing towards. What satisfaction will be gained if Japan joins the company of civilised nations, and if it is numbered among the world powers? This recent victory in war may on the contrary become the source of national ruin, or perhaps even the origin of a great world upheaval. Now is the time we should render our apologies to Heaven for our guilt over the war with Russia, and develop along new paths.

Here Roka directed our minds towards things eternal, and explained that they alone determine the worth of everything.

Victory in war may on the contrary become the source of national ruin, or perhaps even the origin of a great world upheaval.

These words must have been spoken several decades previously, but when I looked at the contemporary world, how well the circumstances seemed to fit, and how dreadfully truthful they were. I did not wish to imagine that Japan might be defeated in the Pacific war. Yet on the other hand I could not avoid being gripped by a presentiment that Japan might end up losing everything, as these words foretold. I felt Roka's utterance bearing down on me like some great prophecy. And with that 'the solemn question, not to be put off for a moment', which he had spoken of, began to pervade my consciousness as the one urgent problem, not permitting any delay.

Gentlemen! The mission of a nation is the mission of a single man. The rules governing the universe are the same as the rules for a man. The aims of the universe must at the same time be the aims of a single man. An individual may be only a tiny drop in the blue sea, yet in all the vastness of the universe he contains something of irreplaceable worth. And is it not truly wretched to be reconciled to our limitations, in an empty void, knowing nothing and comprehending nothing? Just as Japan must now awaken and rise to new life, so must you gentlemen enter into new life here.

This made me realise that even with all the majesty of the universe, there was irreplaceable dignity and worth in each human being, and this brought back again some confidence, replacing my self-loathing.

The past is living in the present, and the present in the future. Time is ceaselessly flowing past, but men never die. Kusunoki Masashige died at Minatogawa, but he lived again and fell again at the entrance to

Port Arthur. Takeo Hirose died on the Fukui Maru, but he is living now in the hearts of all of you. Even while we esteem Admiral Tōgō, we should think about how to properly demonstrate this. We too easily make the mistake of worshipping strength too much, and attempting to show it too formally. That is the way slaves do it, the art of cowards. We must open our own eyes, look squarely at things, and turn to face the right direction. Just as Takeo Hirose is now living in the hearts of you gentlemen, so also are Confucius, Buddha, Christ, and all other heroes, saints, and sages. You must realise that they have become your very blood and sinews, and have shaped your whole beings. Any man without this self-understanding had better quickly kill himself.

He utterly rejected the worship of strength, as something for slaves and cowards, and urged recognition of those precious things which make up our being. 'Any man without this self-understanding had better quickly kill himself.' These words cut my spirit to the quick.

Hot blood will too easily cool in the end. You gentlemen are still on the rising tide, but your life in the flesh will last only a mere 50 or 60 years. All too soon the time will come for today's youthful energy to fade. Yet here is something which will never cool, but burn on with the years and never know age.

Gentlemen! Those who live with the Spirit shall never die. As I step down now from this esteemed platform, I shall conclude by quoting the words spoken by a Hebrew prophet—'They that wait and trust upon Jehovah shall renew their strength; they shall mount up with wings as eagles; they shall run, and not be weary; they shall walk, and not faint.'

This address by Roka Tokutomi exerted considerable influence on me. At the very least it lit a glimmer of light in the inner recesses of my heart. It was a fortunate accident that I discovered this article for it began to shake my sluggish mind into action. If read during peaceful times, it would not have stirred much interest, but here I was grappling with monumental human problems, believing I would never resolve them. So the article took a complete hold on me, and I must have read it repeatedly, thoroughly chewing it over word by word.

Until now I had been dominated by the attitude: what's the use of doing anything, when you have to die anyway? I looked at everything passively and negatively. Those feelings blocked all roads ahead.

But the article proved a turning point and my spirit underwent a great change towards a positive attitude of seeking the truth.

In particular his last sentence, quoted from the Hebrew prophet, burnt its mark deep in my heart. Those words possessed the power to draw my spirit. "Wherever could they have been quoted from?"

I guessed that they probably came from the Old Testament, and for the first time I had a surge of interest in reading the Bible, specifically to find that passage. Of course there was the opposite angle; there's no denying a voice inside warned, "Reading the Bible and all that, you'll end up submitting to Christianity." But for once it was not a matter for simple emotion, about what one liked or disliked; it was no petty matter of saving face. The Bible might happen to be Christian or anything else, but I felt that if truth was truth then one should bravely trust it.

At that time in our compound there was a single leather-bound volume of the Bible in Japanese, containing the Old and New Testaments. Padre Troughton provided it for those who attended his weekly meetings, but it mostly lay unread on the table.

At that time creatures such as missionaries were far from being my favourites, and my self-respect did not allow me to attend the weekly meetings on Christianity. I had no wish to appear as some sort of Christian hypocrite, and regarded them suspiciously and felt reproachful towards the whole business.

So I decided to read the Bible by myself, to make a thorough investigation as to whether this thing called Christianity would truly provide what I sought. Looking back, it was an arrogant attitude; nevertheless just to get as far as reading the Bible was a significant advance, a leap forward. So for the first time in my life I took the Bible in my hands and came face to face with it.

When I finally got that thick Bible consisting of the Old and New Testaments before me, I was stuck, not knowing where those words might be found. There was no way of guessing the best place to start. But at least I had time to spare. If I had to read it, I thought it would probably be interesting to read it once right through. And that thought helped me make up my mind to start reading right from the first page. Thus I launched into the Bible from the first page of the Book of Genesis. Genesis, Exodus, Leviticus... so I went on in sequence through the Old Testament.

It required a lot of perseverance, but was comparatively pleasurable reading, bringing a feeling of contact with a new world. More than anything else, my desire to find those words as quickly as possible drove me forward.

Before long the chilly winter ended and the voice of September called. By stages, spring came to our prison camp. During winter we crouched over stoves, but now we emerged to savour the warm spring sunlight, and this produced a sense of physical relaxation. From now on we took much pleasure in being out in the open air instead of in stuffy huts. Wherever you are, spring is marvellous. Around the doghouses and on our cultivated land, the first sown seeds of flowers, tomatoes, cucumbers and so forth sprouted and, thanks to everyone's earnest labours, grew steadily. Lacking such refinement, I did not put my hand to this laborious business, but mainly went round as a spectator.

Soon the neighbouring wide pastureland took on colour in place of its winter sere, as though the spirit of life had returned to move it. Newborn lambs gambolled in the fields, charming us. They jiggled their tails as they eagerly sought their mothers' teats, and the sight of several lambs frolicking together was uplifting, far more captivating than dogs or cats.

From time to time large flocks of sheep passed along the highway by the southern boundary, guided and protected by shepherds and their sheep dogs. The very picture of serenity, a calm and peaceful rural scene, such as not to be found in Japan.

Dr Bossard, then serving as the New Zealand resident representative of the Swiss-based International Committee of the Red Cross Society, used to come from Auckland to inspect this POW camp once every three months.

Thanks to the Doctor's kind efforts, gradual changes took place to improve our lives. One was the availability of newspapers published in Hawaii for people of Japanese ancestry. The *Hawaii Times, Hawaii Hochi*, and other newspapers, printed half in English and half in Japanese, would be collected into one-week or ten-day lots and sent to camp for us. Regardless of the quality of the magazine or newspaper, the Japanese language was welcome, and all the more so for those who did not know English. We had been starved for news and benefited greatly from these sources of information.

In September and October on the battlefronts of Europe, after the occupation of Sicily, the Allied armies pushed ahead in the liberation of the Italian mainland. References to the American Fifth Army commanded by Lieutenant General Clark and to the British Eighth Army of General Montgomery were often reported in the newspapers.

Thanks to Dr Bossard we were able to see magazines such as *Life*, as well as newspapers. This was a great pleasure; our spare time was filled in, and our brains were largely saved from atrophy.

Also, about this time, each of the compounds set up what the Japanese forces used to call a *shuho*—a canteen or 'PX'. According to the provisions of the POW Convention a POW should receive a certain payment determined according to his rank and work performed. For this purpose, a currency was established circulating only within the camp, and was paid to us each month. It was usually a sum of one pound and so many shillings. Such articles of daily use as tobacco, confectionery, chocolate, chewing gum, soap, and writing paper were provided in the canteen, and we bought them with this currency.

By now spring had reached its height. Yet I kept on without respite reading the Old Testament, on through the Books of Samuel, Kings... Job... Psalms... But I still could not discover the passage which triggered my search.

Meanwhile the day came round marking one full year since I had been taken prisoner. The unforgettable 13 November. And it came so quickly. That night battle at sea one year ago, then the sinking, being adrift, the totally unimagined fate of being taken prisoner... This sequence of events played through my mind as vividly as if they'd happened yesterday. I remembered my comrades who had died. This last year an unimaginable world had gradually unfolded. And now my continued existence became once again a reason for subjecting myself to bitter self-reproach. I thought, is this right of me? When that enemy shell hit us, why had I alone been miraculously saved? If I had simply died then it would have been all over with none of these troubles. I felt this even more strongly now. The more I thought of my dead comrades, the more painful it was to still be living.

Again I felt as if only the worthless cast-off shell of my physical body was alive, due only to human instinct. On the other hand, I was becoming aware that this world was full of ever greater and complicated contradictions. After all, what about world conflict, injustices, wrongs and inequalities? Compared with these, my own individual case was so small as to be insignificant. The more I thought, the less I understood.

Earlier, at the beginning of November, the American forces had landed on the island of Bougainville, our biggest base in the Solomons, near Rabaul. A bitter struggle continued for some time on land, sea and air. The area held many memories, so the reported events had a profound impact on me.

Then a little later, in the last days of November, enemy aircraft-carrier forces launched attacks on Tarawa and Makin in the Gilbert Islands of the central Pacific, and the Marines landed. For the first time, this saw war shifting from the outer southern ocean towards Japan's inner defence lines. The seriousness of the situation was abundantly clear. We worried about how it would turn out, and in the end these islands were captured. Still, the American casualties appeared to have been fairly severe.

The situation of the Allied forces grew ever stronger. Perhaps because of the greater feeling of security this engendered, we sensed the attitude of the prison camp authorities becoming more tolerant.

Meanwhile, in my doghouse, my reading of the Old Testament continued until I reached the Book of Isaiah. It was the first time in my life I had ever encountered such a book, or writings of such splendid power. Then I reached Chapter 40, and right at the end I found the words which had been my goal.

> Those who hope in the LORD will renew their strength. They will soar on wings like eagles; they will run and not grow weary, they will walk and not be faint.

There it was in the Old Testament after all. No one forgets the first words they knew from the Bible. As long as I live I shall not forget the text which first led me there.

Boosted by the joy of my discovery I continued reading the Old Testament, and when I had read it right through, I felt the gain of some indefinable sense of self-confidence. So I commenced reading the New Testament. But the more I read, the more problems arose, and I ended up understanding nothing.

9

From the Abyss

Spring slipped into summer, and in no time the cycle of the four seasons had been completed. As this year in turn entered its twelfth month, day followed day of fine, hot weather.

And so my second Christmas as a POW arrived. In the northern hemisphere Christmas means snow clad winter scenes, but in the southern hemisphere it's the exact opposite, and it was now the height of summer. Our tomato plants had produced plenty of tomatoes, resembling miniature light bulbs, while the other plants were about to burst into flower.

We non-Christian Japanese had no particular experience of Christmas, but it seemed that people of European origin treated it as the happiest time of the year. Most of the soldiers at the prison camp were given leave from Christmas through to New Year, and went home. So the camp was very quiet and inactive. Motorcars drove along the road more frequently than usual, some with Christmas trees loaded on their roofs.

Only the barbed wire palisades formed a boundary between the world of the free, on the one hand, and our existence of captivity, on the other. The fence focused our awareness on the strange contrast.

The army canteen supplied us with plenty of ice cream on Christmas day. We also received presents of confectionery from Padre Troughton, and all spent the evening together in the recreation room. But even Christmas, which was meant to be joyful, was not the least bit happy for me, still troubled by doubts. The jokes and laughter seemed flat. Sorrow lay heavy on my soul.

It must have been just after Christmas Day that the newspapers headlined the appointment of General Eisenhower as commander in chief of the Allied Expeditionary Forces for the landing operations on the European continent.

With Christmas over it was soon another year, and we greeted New Year's Day 1944.

From early morning on New Year's Day an uninterrupted stream of cars flowed from the right to the left along the road in front of the camp. They seemed to be coming from Wellington and heading for some nearby town. The latest models of beautiful passenger cars slipped past pretty much without intermission. At first we thought it must be an emergency, until someone asked one of the camp guards. It turned out there were horse races in a nearby town. We couldn't believe it!

I knew, from movie shows and other sources, that the British passionately followed horse racing, but I was a little disgusted at these races held in the height of a war. Many of their soldiers were risking their lives fighting in the front lines. Surely it was shameful that the nation, well behind the guns, spent their time on horse races? That's the way it looked to me.

The more I thought of it, the more this human world seemed riddled with contradictions.

Before long the flower beds, which our people worked so hard at, blossomed with beautiful flowers: sweet peas, then poppies, marigolds, cosmos, and others... Our drab prison compounds were flooded with soft colours, presenting an indescribably cheerful scene. I had never noticed before that flowers could be so beautiful—another new experience.

Living here we discovered first-hand the benefits of what might be called the simple life. In ordinary times we had attached ourselves to superfluous objects. But here we had doghouses, the necessary minimum of clothing, and plain food... It was a life forced on us by others, but nonetheless entirely liveable.

The sun's heat shimmered in the neighbouring pasture, forcing the flocks of sheep to seek the scanty shade of trees where they lay motionless, panting. Once the newspapers reported the onslaught of a heat wave in parts of Australia, causing great losses of stock. Around the same time we experienced a day like that at the camp.

Strong winds blew down from the hills, drying the ground and whipping up dust storms. Our doghouses, with many cracks and crevices, were overwhelmed by grit, and at night the huts shook and creaked so much that sleep was impossible. These winds came at intervals every few days. Our flowering plants and tomatoes needed the protection of screens, but even then we had a lot of damage. Among the POWs were men from the Joshu district, and from the well-known saying about that area, 'Scorching winds, and scolding women', this local wind got dubbed 'the scorching wind'.

After the first few days of February, a splendid harvest of tomatoes and cucumbers became ripe for our table.

We had never taken a single step outside our compound, but still we had deepened our knowledge about New Zealand. Among the books circulating was one written by a Japanese, entitled *Minami no Risokyo Nyujiirando (New Zealand Southern Utopia)*, and taking this title at face value it must have been a much-blessed place.

New Zealand lies in the sea to the east of Australia. The ocean between is called the Tasman Sea, named after the discoverer of New Zealand, the Dutch explorer Tasman. Among the tobacco they used to supply us with there was one brand named Tasman. The country consists of three islands, the North Island, South Island, and Stewart Island. The combined area is a bit bigger than the Japanese main island of Honshu. Between the North and South islands flows the narrow Cook Strait. This is named after the noted British navigator Cook, who came later than Tasman and annexed the country. The two large cities in the North Island are the capital, Wellington, and Auckland, with Christchurch being the principal city in the South Island.

The climate is oceanic, with little difference between the four seasons, and one could almost say that nearly all the year round it is like autumn.

The principal industries were stock raising and agriculture. The cheif exports were wool, mutton and dairy products. There was little of much consequence produced on the manufacturing side.

The Maori were the original inhabitants, notable for their traditions and customs.

At that time the Labour Party cabinet held office. We heard that the social system of the country was well provided for, with such things as minimum wage rates and state insurance for old age. We were not able to gain any adequate knowledge of the real substance of these things, but their names alone made us envious. We heard that New Zealand was one of the leading countries in such things as the number of motorcars relative to population. The average annual income was fairly high. So the expression 'Southern Utopia' was not altogether an exaggeration.

The population in the 1940s was only some 1.3 million people. With so few people living in such a well-favoured land, what institutions might not be possible? In a place like Japan such things would be out of the question, however much desired. I thought what a contradiction it was that there should be such discrimination in the way the territory of the world was shared. And while these contradictions were much to be deplored, what a crime it was if the countries with plenty to spare should shut out the countries which had insufficient. Even the best of social systems, when seen from the world as a whole, was no more than based on the sacrifice of others.

Having thought it through, I came to the conclusion that this was relatively speaking a problem for the Japanese people themselves. The Japanese people should open their eyes to see things more from the point of view of the people of the world, and should win the confidence of the world. As I saw it, we must go ahead more positively with emigration overseas. On this latter point, it was a matter for some considerable thought that the Chinese had already found their way even into this country, although only as a minority.

Early in February the newspapers reported that American aircraft-carrier forces in vast numbers had attacked the Marshall Islands, our eastern bastions in the southern archipelago. It was reported that they had landed on Wotho and Kwajalein after savage bombing and shelling, and captured them after violent fighting.

We waited anxiously, expecting to hear that our Combined Fleet had at last come out to trade blows with the American fleet, but there was no such news, and this corner of the southern archipelago was all too easily broken away.

We could not help worrying about the future, with the unfathomable expansion of America's immense fighting power threatening to carry the war situation completely before it. A little later there were raids on the islands of Truk, and in the New Guinea area a landing by MacArthur's army in the Admiralty Islands.

At night when I stepped alone out of my hut, a heaven full of stars would shine beautifully in the jet-black night sky. Among them the Southern Cross was the most impressive.

This latitude was further south than the Cape of Good Hope at the southern extremity of Africa; we had come far. The constellation of Orion could also be seen. One after the other, memories of past times at sea would return. The constellations of the heavens are integral to a seafarer's being, and as I reviewed my short lifetime and reflected that I had probably said farewell forever to a sea-going life, I felt desolate.

The light shone dully from many outside sources, illuminating the grounds of the prison camp ringed with barbed wire. The neighbouring paddocks slept in darkness, and all around was hushed and quiet. Everything was still. Few people in the wide world would be aware of our existence. In this place people like us were no more than creatures thrown aside from real events.

In contrast to the grandeur of the whole world and the whole universe, one's own frailty came to be clearly felt. Yet while on the one hand one was struck by a sense of personal frailty, questions welled up on the other hand about what would happen to the world; what path would world history follow? Since we had been taken prisoner my hopes grew that I could fathom how all this would turn out.

About this time, we gained a new plaything in the recreation room— billiards. A man from the New Zealand Red Cross Society, who had previously visited our compound, had been moved by the bleak recreation room and, through a friend, had presented some billiard balls. Our officer colleagues from the Engineering Branch promptly put their talents to use and knocked together a small billiard table. The YMCA sent us a number of second-hand cues and the table was set up.

Here the story takes a turn. My reading through the Bible, which had commenced about the previous September, had been in a state of suspension since the beginning of this year. I had set to reading with enormous vigour, helped by a flourishing spirit of inquiry, but by the time I had finished the Old Testament and had commenced the New Testament I had become a little tired and sated. Moreover, the book contained ways of expressing things that were far removed from commonsense, such as miracle stories, and one's eye was always coming across passages which were incomprehensible to human reason. All sorts of obstacles blocked my way. So my enthusiasm wore down and I gradually drifted away. Again I reflected that belief in Christianity seemed too difficult for me to grasp alone.

But there was another aspect. Since the beginning of this year another problem arose. It had been there since way back, but until now had been put to one side. It gained weight with time.

The problem was my tobacco smoking. Until captured, I had been able to enjoy my cigarettes as freely as I wanted. But as a POW I came under restrictions. In the early period I received a paltry ration of five cigarettes per day, and could no longer smoke as freely as I liked. Strangely enough, the human reaction to restriction is to crave even more.

I have already described how many of the POWs debased themselves because of their addiction. Although I had not acted similarly, there had been no difference in the way I felt.

Going through this small business about smoking, I saw how much it besmirched a person's self-respect and I became disgusted with myself. At times I fell into strong self-hatred. A trifling thing such as smoking bound a man, governed and enslaved him. I longed to escape from these shackles.

I thought how fresh and fine it would be to give up tobacco, to feel no compulsion to smoke. I prayed from the depths of my soul for help to overcome the vice.

As usual, while one side of my mind resolved to give up tobacco, the other side raised objections: "Surely there isn't anything the least bad about tobacco. Really, why do you need to brood so much? Smoke it! Smoke it as much as you like..."

Why had I become so obsessed? I had to admit it was all very strange. Surely, smoking itself could not in any way be considered a sin. Nor is it touched on in any way in the Bible. One simply cannot attach arbitrary significance to it.

Still I felt like replying, "Yes of course, but on this occasion, just this once, won't you grant me any solution?" and "Here I am praying to give it up, so why can't I?"

My lack of will power exasperated me. Until now I had simply assumed that I would be able to manage anything through strength of will. But when I tried to overcome a critical problem, I simply couldn't.

I gave up tobacco for several days at a time but could not keep it up for long. It always ended in failure, only a three-day penitent. I doubted whether will power had any value at all. In the end I suspected that everyone was like me, weak-willed and with no self-respect.

Ultimately something extra is needed and I gradually realised what. The problem of my addiction was merely a symptom of a bigger problem affecting my whole existence. If I can't solve even this, then I'm quite useless and beyond saving. But if I could solve this... how fine it would be. And perhaps this would fix all my other problems at the same time, I thought. With these ups and downs, my mental war intensified daily.

Before long the warm summer passed, and March and April heralded the return of autumn.

All the plants withered away and their remnants were removed. The compounds became dreary again. As autumn deepened, we resumed our places beside the stove, and around it the unfading flowers of conversation bloomed. Now and then we chopped wood to put in the stove. But from long lack of physical work our strength had gone and we were hardly up to it.

Our tedious idle life continued, permeated by an anguishing spirit. The business about wanting to give up tobacco intensified the strife in my mind.

In these circumstances the Bible, temporarily laid aside, was taken up again and serious reading resumed. Perhaps because of the interval of a few months, the words showed themselves to me in a new light.

Having nothing to do, we often dived straight into bed after the evening meal and shower. By now the dark evenings came early. Junior Lieutenant Hirahashi, a pilot from the Reserve Training School, occupied the bed next to mine. The same insurmountable problems troubled us both. At times we opened our hearts to each other in conversation, but we were a pair who had not yet found the truth, and our conversation never emerged above a certain level. We were halfway men, lacking ultimate conviction.

The nights wore on, but sleep didn't come quickly. In fact, my mind became more lucid. Outside lights penetrated through a little glass window above my feet into the dark interior of the room. Quiet nights, rainy nights, windy nights, many a night I spent in the dark hut absorbed in quiet contemplation, groaning within. Only at these times was I truly honest with myself.

As I lay there, I gradually became conscious that a dark bottomless void wrapped around me—a vast emptiness, black and impenetrable. The more I became aware of this pit, the more minuscule the image of my own self became. I began to sense the proportion of my small identity in this vast emptiness.

I knew that I was all alone in the universe. I knew that there was not a single person in this whole world on whom I could rely. I stood there by myself and noticed how insignificant—like foam that emerges and vanishes—was the transient human form. I was weak, weak, all too weak. Was this a Japanese? Was this a fighting man of Japan? From deep in my mind a voice of scorn reviled me and I wept. Where was the solution?

I never dreamt of receiving forgiveness for my weakness through cheap human sympathy. But I also understood that if forgiveness didn't come, then humankind was subject to eternal despair. Man couldn't resolve it so it must be resolved by something else. Having sunk to the lowest depths, I could at least understand that much. Therefore, this forgiveness must be given elsewhere.

It must have been then that the cross of Jesus Christ first came to be present in the depths of my soul... As time passed this became gradually more conscious, drawing closer to me. This was an entirely new experience. It was as though a straying traveller had lost his way in utter darkness, and had spotted in the far distance a single gleam of light. I discovered that single point of light. And most wonderful, before long, tears of anguish had changed to tears of inexpressible happiness. I certainly experienced a great change of mind as I lay in that dark hut.

But even in recognising this, I was not yet able to immediately acknowledge faith in Jesus Christ. To make an attitude of formal belief in Christianity clear to everyone required courage, and obstacles still lay in my way.

The first was whether belief in Christianity was contrary to the basic nature of Japanese nationality. In the light of later knowledge, it is clear that this is not the case, but for us who bore traditional Japanese conceptions this still caused pain. Whatever happened I wanted to be one who loved his mother country Japan, and thus some time was needed before the false myths of my education could be cleared away.

An even greater obstacle lay elsewhere. Would belief in Jesus Christ be something that depended generally on my own strength? Or would it be entirely through strength from elsewhere, through surrendering my entire self to Jesus Christ? That was the question. In this I wished to have some sort of strength of my own acknowledged. To depend on and cling unconditionally and blindly to anybody would seem to be an act fitting for people lacking in self-respect—weaklings and illiterates. I thought of faith in a manner half depending on strength from elsewhere and half on one's own strength. Whichever way it was to be, I still wished to find in the act of faith a place for my own strength. I just could not abandon myself entirely, or give up everything I knew.

The author in 1942, the year he was taken prisoner near Guadalcanal.
(photo courtesy of the author)

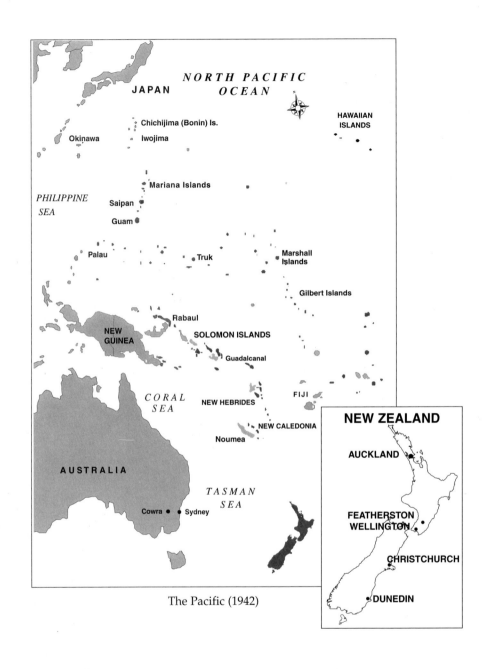

The Pacific (1942)

Guard tower, Featherston Camp. *(photo courtesy of Noel L Earles)*

View of Featherston Camp overlooking the camp hospital in the centre of the picture, with No.2 compound behind and No.4 compound beyond. *(photo courtesy of Noel L Earles)*

General view of Featherston Camp, showing barbed wire boundary fences.
(photo courtesy of Noel L Earles)

'Doghouse' huts within the camp of the type that served as
accommodation for the prisoners and guards.
(photo courtesy of Alexander Turnbull Library, John Pascoe Collection)

A prisoner on cleaning duties. *(photo courtesy of Noel L Earles)*

A Japanese prisoner speaking with a prison guard.
(photo courtesy of Alexander Turnbull Library, John Pascoe Collection)

A prison guard shares a light with a prisoner.
(photo courtesy of Alexander Turnbull Library, John Pascoe Collection)

Japanese prisoners planting cabbages in the state market gardens near the camp.
(photo courtesy of Alexander Turnbull Library, John Pascoe Collection)

An elephant carved by a Japanese prisoner. *(courtesy of Noel L Earles)*

Rev. Hessell W.F. Troughton, the chaplain at Featherston.
(photo courtesy of Alison Smith and Doreen Payne)

Padre Troughton's Christian group in the officers' compound. Back row, left to right: Senior Lieutenant Sakujiro Kamikubo (engineering); Air Service Pilot Masaru Izumisawa; Junior Lieutenant Toshio Adachi. Front row, left to right: Junior-Lieutenant Sadamu Ito; Lieutenant Michiharu Shinya; Air Service Pilot Tokuchiyo Hirahashi; Daizo Ikebuchi (officers' cook).

(photo courtesy of Noel L Earles)

The prisoners leave Featherston Camp bound for Japan on December 30 1945.
(photo courtesy of Noel L Earles)

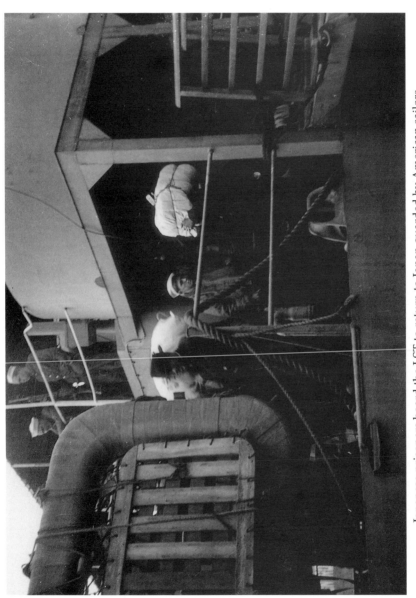

Japanese prisoners board the LST to return to Japan guarded by American sailors.
(photo courtesy of Noel L Earles)

The author and Mrs Shinya, Yokohama, 2000. *(photo courtesy of the author)*

10

Life Transformed

April 1944 was nearly past when I came down with a chill, making me listless. I lay in bed for two or three days by myself in my doghouse. I didn't think anything particular of it, but just couldn't shake it off. One day the commandant, on his mid-morning round of inspection, spotted me and gave instructions for me to be attended to.

A medical orderly arrived promptly, examined me, and took away a blood sample. He soon returned with the surprising information that I had malaria, and that I had to go into hospital for about two weeks of treatment. There had been no symptoms at all previously and I could not imagine why malaria should have flared up. Even now I did not have a severe fever or overpowering bouts of shivering.

But no sooner said than done, I was admitted to the adjoining hospital that same day.

The hospital ward was quiet and clean with individual rooms, soft beds and pristine white sheets—a much superior level of living than in our doghouses. The day was chilly and cloudy, but with steam heating laid on it was snug in the ward. On top of that, the medical orderlies treated me like an honoured guest, extending every courtesy, and I became rather self-conscious about moving in.

Just as it turned dark that evening, a middle-aged civilian called in to see me. He came in bowing at first, in the most diffident manner, as though he was going to start by saying something, but he just opened a suitcase and laid out the contents on the bed—a Japanese inkstone with an ink stick and writing brush. There was also a book of woodblock prints of the Tokugawa Era. Apparently he hoped to cheer us up by showing these. For my part I did not feel the slightest interest in such things, but was touched by the kind thoughts of this man who wanted somehow to console us.

Before long he tried to open a conversation. His first words, which I had been waiting for, came out:

"Do you have a wife?"

"No." My reply was very simple, even rather abrupt.

"Well then, perhaps you have a fiancee?"

With all this talk about wives and fiancees, it seemed he had no idea of the turmoil in my mind.

"No." My reply was the same as before. Putting myself in his place, I would have liked to have said "Yes", but a fact is a fact. Then came the next question:

"Well then, perhaps you have a girlfriend?"

This was his final trump card. It would sound too pathetic to answer 'No' to this also. Our first conversation would be quite spoilt. But even at that, there had been in my past no particular girlfriend either. So then, much helped by sympathy, I said:

"Well, sort of."

Hearing this reply seemed at last to put his mind at rest.

"Oh!" he said. (This exclamation is typical among them.) "That is good. When the war is over and you return to Japan, you should have a wife and live happily."

What delightful words those were. Enough to make one cheer up. But immediately other words, "What are you talking about? You don't know a man's mind!" came to the tip of my tongue. My life was already finished. Any idea of 'when the war is over and you return to Japan' was no more than words in a dream.

He finally presented me with a pencil, and went his way.

Yet however it might have seemed, I cannot forget his good intentions, or his love. That there should be on this earth even one person willing to humble himself to notice me, an outcast among humankind, and willing to greet me warmly like an old friend, was a marvel providing boundless consolation. It was an encouragement and source of strength to me. As I learnt later, he ran a radio business in a nearby town, and was a Christian of the Society of Friends. They said he came to the hospital occasionally to visit the Japanese POWs. With him it was a case of literally putting into practice those words of Jesus Christ, 'Love your enemies', even in the middle of a war. Although his activities were perhaps trifling and not worthy of notice, through them he became a person I shall never forget.

The day after my admission to hospital they gave me quinine—morning, noon and night—in such doses as were hard to take. In three or four days my stomach became completely upset. All day long I browsed through the magazines that the medical orderlies brought me.

After about a week my friend Junior Lieutenant Hirahashi visited, bringing two or three books, and we talked of various things. Among the books was one *Heimin no Fukuin* (*The Gospel for the Common People*) written by Gunpei Yamamuro of the Salvation Army in Japan, and a pamphlet *The Reason Why* by Robert Laidlaw, a Christian said to be manager of a large department store in Auckland. These introductions to Christianity were helpful in leading me to a deeper understanding of the faith.

Finally I was driven to the brink of either believing or not believing in Jesus Christ. I came to the conclusion that there was no other path but to believe in him. It was clear too that in human weakness, a human being cannot stand alone without the Absolute and only God. But for all that, I could not make the one final decision. I just could not renounce this thing called Self. The more I tried, the stronger was my attachment to my ego. Wouldn't it mean giving up everything? Face-saving and self-esteem tagged along after me to the very end.

One day Padre Troughton came to visit me. Until now I had not liked meeting him too much, and kept him at a distance as much as possible. But this time he made a direct approach to me which broke my stubborn mind.

I can't recollect the conversation we exchanged then, but I remember that he spoke briefly about salvation through Jesus Christ. His voice was quiet but carried a powerful conviction, and I felt an authority that was hard to defy. Intense emotions filled my mind. It was not just the Padre speaking but, more than that, through the Padre I felt as though Jesus Christ was living and beginning to speak to me directly. This sacred authority overwhelmed my ugly egotism and I bitterly regretted my perfunctory and distrustful attitude towards the Padre. I was finally given the will to renounce those last tenacious beliefs.

The special treatment for malaria took about half a month and, once completed, I was discharged from hospital.

Then a few days later, on 12 May, there was a Bible study meeting held in our compound, and on that day I began regular attendance.

After many twists and turns, this day became a milestone for me, for I decided that the path of Jesus Christ was my life's path, and I chose to follow it. The bearings for my course in life were fixed that day. There was nothing special about that particular meeting, but I felt as though a great load had been dropped from my shoulders, and felt some indefinable sense of gladness. But still my tobacco addiction remained, and it hung over me like unfinished business. But then something happened three days later on 15 May.

The day closed without incident; it was evening. Several of our colleagues had gathered in my hut and were debating vigorously. Then due to some direct motivation which I can't remember, the thought hit me: I have now given up tobacco! I had been led spontaneously to this state. The inner impediment was completely removed, and in its place I felt a new strength filling me, a natural feeling that my hands would keep away from tobacco. "I've got it!" burst out like a cry of victory. I experienced liberation from long bondage. What inexpressible freedom and strength flooded my heart. Joy! Joy! Joy! From that moment I truly and positively experienced new life in Jesus Christ.

From the next day on everything was transformed. Everything had been made new. Now even death would not matter! This way I could have what I had wanted so keenly. At last I could grasp what I had been seeking so long. My whole being was governed by a feeling of relief, with all things surrendered in trust. I had come through a path of anxiety, agitation, doubt and darkness. But now I could tread with my feet planted firmly and strongly on the earth. What mental suffering I had been through. But the deeper my suffering had been, the greater now was my happiness.

To think of it calmly, here I was only 24-years-old. Looking back, how long I seemed to have suffered. But then looking again, how quickly I had come through it all. The rest of my life had been handed back to me.

Our position as POWs was a sad one. We had no assurance of being allowed to live in the days ahead, and not one hopeful thing could be seen for our future. But, in the middle of all this, nothing could snatch away the peace which now captivated my heart. There in the POW camp with its apparent restrictions, I came to experience complete freedom through faith in Jesus Christ. It could be said that only the external restraint of the prison camp fences brought the opportunity for true internal freedom. In this way a POW camp changed into a unique paradise on earth. That is no exaggerated statement. An entirely new life opened up there.

Beyond that, faith in the Bible gave true and correct sight in understanding and perception of this present world. I felt that the general problems of life would be solved one by one. My doubts and perplexities faded away.

In this way faith in Jesus Christ set me free, and gave me strength and clarity of thought. It was now a case of—let them come with all their arrows and guns.

Changes occurred both inside and outside the prison camp. In early June the newspapers reported how the Allied Expeditionary Forces under the command of General Eisenhower crossed the English Channel and effected their historic landing on the coast of Normandy in France. This is worthy of record as one of the great climaxes of the Second World War, probably its greatest highlight. Its date had been awaited so long and anxiously that even in our isolated prison camp we couldn't help being excited. We mentally grasped our sweating hands in suspense waiting to see which side would win.

Following that was the American attack against Saipan in the Mariana Islands in the Pacific. The landing commenced with support from powerful sea and air forces. One could not help being caught up in admiration for this magnificent style of warfare. From the Gilberts to the Marshalls, from the Marshalls to the Marianas, it seemed like a heavy tank going ahead and crushing all before it. I could see clearly in my mind's eye lovely and peaceful Saipan and the quiet town of Garapan, where we had made port several times during the war. Before long, in July, Tinian and Guam also became the scenes of enemy landings, and the strategic bases in those Central Pacific islands passed into enemy hands. These later became the centres of B-29 operations, but in those days no one could have imagined that these would become in a reverse way the greatest bases for air raids against the Japanese mainland. One had a profound feeling that the initiative in the war had already passed to the Americans. Compared with one or two years previously, the situation on the battlefronts of both Europe and the Pacific had completely changed course.

In our compounds many of the men were preoccupied with cultivating the soil in their garden plots, awaiting the arrival of our second spring. These areas had been greatly extended compared with the previous year, and many varieties of seed had been sown. As the days passed the seeds put out their shoots, and growth commenced. This year one of the officers serving in the camp brought us some strawberry seedlings early in the season; these had been planted and their fruit was awaited with pleasure.

Five months after that epoch-making day that divided my life in two, several of us from our group were baptised by Padre Troughton. I remember how the Padre put water in a red-lacquered wooden bowl he had brought back from Japan, and how after saying some words he dipped his hand in the water, and laid that hand on my head. The action was not without a feeling of some formality, much ritualism, and strangeness. Yet I felt glad that with this I had clearly become one of Christ's people. Now that I had been distinctly marked before all men, I felt that there could be no drawing back.

After this there was also the celebration of Holy Communion. It was my first time with this ceremony, eating a finely cut piece of bread and the drinking of a minute quantity of grape wine, and I hardly knew what it was all about. I felt it to be even more formal than the rite of Baptism.

Ordinary people might have regarded being baptised by an enemy pastor unpatriotic conduct. For the times, that was only to be expected. That I might be so regarded was most regrettable to me. But now I was no longer afraid of anybody, for I knew that the essence of Christianity by no means lay in such things, but that it was faith in Christianity which would make us truly human, truly Japanese and truly patriots in the strictest sense.

The great majority of the men in the POW camp remained firm believers in Japanese traditions and customs, and the material world. They lived through force of habit without taking even one step to break away; in the same way I, too, had seen things only superficially and had not sought the truth. Vainly and complacently I had mouthed things about Japan and patriotism, without troubling myself deeply. Now I was shamefully aware of the extent of my foolishness.

I was no longer bewitched by that beautiful word 'patriotism'. How ignorant and blind we had been until now. I myself had loved Japan without limit. I had burned with an ardent desire to show my love in some way. For this very reason I had enrolled in the Naval Academy, hoping for a chance to do my best for our country. I think no mistake lay in those motives. But once I came to reflect on them, I realised that I had been greatly mistaken in the manner of their expression. Japan had sought to make its collective national entity into something absolute. My patriotism and the patriotism of others had expressed itself in conceited and madly mistaken beliefs. We had believed that Japan was the indestructible and invincible land of the gods, that the Emperor was a god present as man, and that Japan was the centre of the whole eight-cornered universe. It had taken me so long to realise the error of these things.

I was long troubled over whether or not Christianity conflicted with the Japanese entity. I did not wish to become a spineless 'cosmopolitan'. Come what may, I wished to be Japanese in the truest sense. How then could these two things be made compatible? That is what I sought.

When I came to understand Christianity, I learnt that it is this very faith in the Bible which makes us into citizens of the world in the most correct sense, while at the same time it makes us members of our own nations. When I awoke to faith in the one God who is Father of humankind, I first grasped fully that all people under this God are truly brothers and sisters. I ceased to think of the Japanese as a special superior race, or that British and Americans were something quite different. I knew now that Japanese and Americans, white men and black men, were essentially without any distinction before God. All of us, without exception, are equally human; nobody is inferior or superior. I learnt that the life of an individual is something precious and irreplaceable before God.

Until now we hadn't understood the true meaning of human dignity. In fact when I considered it this way, I realised that in Japan there have been few 'patriots' in the true sense, and few 'citizens of the world' either.

11

God's Calling

The days and months piled up. We adjusted to our conditions, accepting them as a matter of course—a marked change compared to when first captured. Occasionally a fresh realisation startled me and I would be compelled to reflect on my direction. But circumstance and the passage of time were our masters, assimilating us to the normal run of life.

Our lives improved further through the efforts of Dr Bossard, the Swiss delegate of the International Committee of the Red Cross, when we were allowed to see movie shows—a significant event!

There was already a 16 mm cinema projector in the camp, for the New Zealand soldiers' entertainment, and this became available for our use. It was transported from the soldiers' quarters by motor vehicle and operated in our recreation rooms.

On the first occasion they screened travel films about New Zealand, and newsreels. It was as though we had suddenly come back into the human world. There were views of the volcano Mount Taranaki, hot springs at Rotorua, the Maori, notable species of ferns, and the vast spreading pasture landscapes. Of especially deep interest were the Maoris, about whom we had already learnt a certain amount. There were a number of men of Maori origin among the soldiers at the prison camp, and they had become especially friendly with us. Their skin was much browner than ours. As a rule they were good-natured men, and in various ways had much in common with the Japanese.

The movie screenings took place once every two weeks. Needless to say, these shows gave us all the greatest of pleasure. On subsequent occasions the enlisted men's wishes were met by the screening of love stories. There is really no limit to what people expect!

Original amateur dramatic shows were also being staged, in the enlisted men's and construction workers' compounds. Tired of the commonplace entertainment, they demanded proper performances with meaning and elaborate presentation. As well as the theatrical activities, something like an orchestra had been organised, which performed popular songs.

In the general atmosphere it seemed that most of us felt that we might as well live out this POW life happily and pleasantly, as no one knew how long it would last. We had theatrical competitions, mah-jong tournaments, *shogi* tournaments, all coming in succession.

In the Pacific war campaigns, Saipan, Tinian, and Guam were wiped out first, then in September Palau was captured. In October American carrier-borne air forces wrought havoc on Okinawa, Taiwan and Luzon. Then at last about 20 October the American recapture of Leyte Island in the Philippines commenced with the support of several powerful fleets. General MacArthur had fled from Corregidor off Bataan Peninsula earlier, but now trod again on the soil of the Philippine Islands.

The war had turned completely on history's stage. We worried as the tide of events each day took a more unfavourable turn for the Japanese side. The newspaper showed photographs of the battleships of the Yamato class, and others of the memorable Japanese fleet, caught in battle. We did not yet know the facts, but the Japanese Navy had suffered some annihilating blows. These large-scale enemy landing operations followed each other in rapid succession, and our conversation concerned where the next landing was likely to be. We felt the first premonitions that the war might end earlier than expected.

The outside world underwent these violent changes while we quietly continued our weekly Bible study meetings.

This was the most pleasant occasion each week. Five or six of us would spread around the ping-pong table, sing hymns together, and listen to the Padre talking about the Bible. As he spoke unpractised Japanese, he would always come with a manuscript prepared in advance, with Japanese written in Romanised script. It was no small matter that he went to the trouble of making such preparations. What he had to say was elementary and couldn't be considered profound, but it was at a time when we felt a ravenous appetite for the Bible and we all listened eagerly.

At these meetings Padre Troughton often said, in his characteristic accent, "A person who has been saved should pass it on to others also." Perhaps he uttered these words casually—I did not think anything special of them at first—but eventually the phrase struck a strong response in my heart. From then on I knew that I should not keep this faith in the Bible to myself.

Looking back, it could be said that I had simply been intoxicated with joy that I had been saved from a sinful existence. But once that stage passed, and the time for reflection arrived, I realised that my responsibility was surely to pass on to others this joy in faith and assurance. I suspected that this would be a heavy burden because of my reticence and naturally retiring disposition. On the one hand I wished to remain silent, but on the other hand a force was working against this. A new mental struggle arose.

Although there were some 800 Japanese POWs in the camp, why were there so few who believed in Christianity? In the whole camp there must have been a mere ten or so men who acknowledged faith in Jesus Christ. Why had not more people been saved? Could not Christianity save all of humanity wholesale?

I thought that perhaps the truths of Christianity were a profound and high-level matter, requiring some degree of knowledge and perception from those who wished to enter. But that is only one aspect. It does not relate to the essence of the faith. Faith is such that even the most unlearned should be able to enter into it. Well then, why don't they?

People are attached to belief in themselves, to a mistaken overconfidence in human nature, and to their own pride. When we think how strongly rooted and stubborn this is, we realise how difficult it is for people to accept a belief based on the Bible. I could not take any sweet and optimistic view of basic human nature. Rather the opposite, I looked on the human condition as one of despair. That being so, I came to think it unlikely that more than a minority would ever believe in Christianity.

'A person who has been saved should pass it on to others also.' The Padre's voice was never far from my conscience, often making itself heard to pierce me from within. I must do something, I thought to myself, I must do something to pass on the Gospel of Jesus Christ. This feeling gradually ripened in my mind, until at length it impelled me into action.

Our compound possessed several volumes of the works of Toyohiko

Kagawa, in English translation, one among them being his *Christ and Japan*. This was a very simple book written in a popular style intended for the common man. So I decided to translate this back again into Japanese for all the others to read. As I wasn't a confident speaker, I secretly prayed that my doing this might be of some use.

I had no daily obligations to speak of, therefore ample time. So I shut myself away in my doghouse, sitting alone at my desk, and plugged away at the translation. Anything and everything else was forgotten and the hours thus spent were the most pleasant of all. It was my first such experience, and I wasn't able to translate as well as I'd expected. Although I realised it was a faltering and clumsy translation, it was a pleasure to make some progress with the work each day.

This period brought the completion of the second full year since I had been taken prisoner. How quickly those two years flew by. Once again the events of that past day came to mind, and in particular memories of those who had died. I compared myself with them and reflected on my continuing life. I had at last been touched by the Bible, and through that had been granted faith, and had learned that through God and through Jesus Christ men are made to truly live. This was surely the greatest of joys.

I must live only through God, and only for God's sake. However much we wish to do so, as long as we continue to live this physical life, we instinctively seek fulfilment of our bodily needs. Whichever way you look at it, there is no way of insulating ourselves entirely from a way of life centred on the self. If one wanted to get away from that, there was nothing else for it but to die as quickly as possible.

Could death still be the best course for me? I continued to suffer lingering doubts.

Spring had already reached its height. In the warm sunshine various flowering plants sprouted and swelled visibly. This year the gardens had been extended again and everything flourished. So many strawberries ripened that we stuffed ourselves with them. A double-flowered cherry tree sapling had been sent and planted in our compound and with the coming of spring it now blossomed. Although producing only a few flowers they reminded us of Japan.

Meanwhile I finally completed my translation, such as it was, just before Christmas. I hastened to circulate it among the others. To what extent it was read, and what benefit it may have been, I have no means of knowing.

Yet achieving this little task taught me many things, and I was very thankful for the experience. More than that, an inner spirit of passionate devotion to our mother country grew ever stronger, through Jesus Christ.

While engrossed in this work, our second Christmas as captives came round.

This year the members of the church in Wellington with which Padre Troughton was associated had sent Christmas cards, and these were distributed among us. They were only simple things, but one felt in them the touch of a deep love. When I pictured these unseen people, I was struck by the realisation that when we are in the Lord Jesus Christ we humans are all one brotherhood across national boundaries. Warm-hearted Mrs Troughton generously sent a Christmas cake made with her own hands. Christmas presents came from the interpreter Mr Robertson, Dr Bossard, and the Swiss Consul.

I wondered how it was that Christmas could unite us all, in spite of our racial differences and national viewpoints. But thinking further, it was rather, why must the world be roused to furious war and be engaged in mutual slaughter? One was struck again by the incomprehensibility, and one grieved over the deep guilt of humankind.

The day was fairly hot, shelter from the sun necessary. As with last year, the army canteen supplied ice cream. Surpassing all these things, my mind was ruled by the boundless and deep grace and peace of God in the Lord Jesus Christ, the reality restoring and continuing my life.

On the European battlefronts the Allied armies had, since their Normandy landings, already covered a lot of ground and were slowly pushing the German armies back. Then, around Christmas, came the famous counter-attack by the Germans in the Ardennes. For a while confusion reigned between the two sides, and the battle could have gone either way. In the end the Allied armies stemmed the tide. Hitler's last throw was frustrated, and after that no counter-attack worth the name was ever effected.

With the New Year it was now 1945 and the procession of beautiful cars flowing past signified horse races again in the nearby town.

As the year began I took on a new task, starting to translate *The Greatest Thing in the World*, from the pen of the Scotsman, Henry Drummond, who had been a noted scholar and preacher. This recorded how, from the 13th Chapter of the First Letter to the Corinthians in the New Testament, he once gave expression to his great faith in a truly wonderful sermon.

Rich in inspiration and suggestion but relatively short, it taught much about this thing called Christian 'love'. A short while before that, a Christian serving as an officer at the prison camp had lent me a copy of the book.

As POWs we were not free to read any book we chose, and were naturally restricted in our selection. So of course we had no choice but to read the same book any number of times over. This was an unavoidable compulsion imposed from without, but I think it was an advantage to be able thus to read a book with appreciation. One's desire was strengthened to read and learn more widely and plentifully and at a higher level. We had to be satisfied with what was available and thus learned to make do. This was a great strength to me and cause for thankfulness. After all, the one Bible was sufficient.

The cinema shows once every two weeks remained the greatest common pleasure. On one occasion the Swiss Consul lent us films—a Swiss travel movie of picturesque scenery, and one about watch manufacturing. Among the many films, few remained long in my memory. Of these, some which made a deep impression and stimulated me were films introducing the British cities of learning, Edinburgh and Cambridge. The flavour of ancient traditions established over long ages caught my imagination. I have never felt such a burning passion for scholarship as when I watched that screen. If it were permitted, I should like to immerse myself in studies again, I thought. A world of higher learning beckoned. But, as usual, a voice nagged, "Such a thing would be a luxury." To pursue my own interests and study, while many of my wartime comrades had lost their lives, struck me as an inexcusable sin.

While I was contemplating such carefree luxuries, many people struggled to stay alive... But perhaps due to the inherent search for improvement, my yearning for study continued to grow stronger every day.

On the whole, what did I learn in the navy? The experience taught me much, no mistake about that. The strict discipline and thorough training would benefit any education. In that sense I think that training in the armed forces contained much of value but I also realise it contained many defects. One, which became apparent at the camp, was the way we had been pampered. Although not overly knowledgeable, had we not been taught to lord it over others?

In the armed forces the system of rank held absolute authority. It is no exaggeration to say that everything else was sacrificed to that single distinction. No account was taken of the abilities or worth of individual men. The majority would show off their rank, and then be reduced to servility before the rank of others. What crimes have not been committed taking refuge behind rank, or shielded by it? That sort of fighting men's ignorance and arrogance became so obvious as to be unbearable. It was wretched too that I had been so simple-minded about it.

But now I knew the Bible, I learnt through it to be humble before the truth. And then the desire arose to study these Scriptures deeply. We didn't know whether we would be able to return to Japan. But if permitted, how greatly I wished to study the Bible and, if possible, to enrol in a theological college. I felt certain that one day this would come to pass. There could be no other path in life for me. If I could not live for Jesus Christ and for him alone, there would be no value in living any other way.

One day Padre Troughton came into our compound with two Americans. The one who appeared to be the guest of honour possessed a dignified physique and kindly face. He engaged us in conversation for a short while and told us how he had been to Japan before the war. From what I heard later, this man was Dr Decker, a leading figure of the Christian Church in America. I could not understand why he should have come to visit this remote place, but could feel that behind it there was something of the love of Jesus Christ at work.

The interpreter, Lieutenant Robertson, was considerate in his dealings with the Japanese POWs. Although there were those who sometimes made unreasonable requests of him, he showed kindness even in the smallest tasks. Consequently, his conduct brought antagonism from other officers on the enemy side. They complained, "You don't have to be that kind to the Japanese."

This attitude was understandable in people of an enemy country, quite natural. However, his rejoinder was effective and worth savouring. "If it were the other way round and you were a POW in Japan, how would you wish to be treated?" These words made a deep impression on me. When confronted by them, any sort of hostile feeling can only be disarmed. They demonstrated Christian love, which always holds firmly to that which is good overcomes evil.

After mid-February that year, the newspapers reported that American aircraft-carrier forces had executed air raids on the whole Kanto region, and then that several Marine divisions had commenced landing operations on Iwojima. At the end of March bold large-scale operations developed, aimed at the capture of Okinawa, and landings commenced there at the beginning of April. One felt that the Pacific war had truly reached full tide, but the colour of the crisis was black.

On the battle lines in Europe, the Allied armies reached the line of the River Rhine at the end of March; crossings followed in rapid succession and they were breaking through to the final stage. The sudden death of President Roosevelt was reported a little later, about mid-April.

The outcome of the Okinawa battles was decided by the end of April, while at the same time on the European battlefronts, Germany's collapse was imminent. Caught between pincer attacks from the west and the east, the German battle lines were already in confusion, and the fate of Berlin was awaited from morning to evening.

12

The War's End

The German capital Berlin fell at last on 2 May before the crushing offensive of the Russian Army pushing in from the east. Then on 7 May the German armies on the western front made their complete and unconditional surrender to the West European Allied armies. Thus the dramatic final curtain fell, and Hitler and his Nazi empire vanished from the face of the earth.

That same day or the next, early in the morning just about our time of rising, sirens began to sound from Featherston. They emanated from several places, with high and low notes mingling indistinctly through the quiet morning air, and it seemed they would never stop. I wondered what could those sirens be for at this time of day? Could they mean that Germany has surrendered? Such a premonition flashed through my mind. What an indescribably moving moment!

My feelings at the time were of relief, simply full of the feeling that this was just as well. Perhaps in reaction against the thorough destruction and slaughter which had continued for so long, any feeling of victory or defeat was transcended, and I genuinely felt happy at the return of peace. The war, which had looked like going on forever, was half finished, and tension in the camp eased.

Germany's defeat imprinted the stern verdict of history in my mind. Looking back, I remembered how active Hitler had been, how mighty the national strength of Nazi Germany had seemed, and again, how orderly and methodical his totalitarian state. Our generation had turned its adoring eyes to Germany and the German people, but now not a single trace of this remained. I did not think the Anglo–American democratic alliance was entirely in the right, but at least I appreciated the uncertain future for those who take up arms in war. Defeat plainly taught us the sad fate of so-called heroes, and the real facts about them. We had recently seen the wretched death of Mussolini, but he and Hitler were really appalling people. How tragic it was for states and nations to be led by such despots.

By now no one dreamt that Japan would be able to win the war. The outcome became clear—immediate termination would be best, to save the sacrifice of even one more life in this now futile engagement. I began to pray from my heart that it might soon be over.

The wheel of history took its great turn, and we calmly awaited the world which would follow. Inside the prison camp, I took to reading the Old Testament through once again from the beginning.

I understood it more easily the second time. Some books in it such as the Psalms, Jeremiah and others, spoke to my soul in a profound way. Above all, the Book of Isaiah took a decided grip on my mind. Perhaps because Isaiah was so appropriate to my present condition, it struck home. The style was truly beautiful, powerful and majestic. I loved this book most deeply of all the books in the Old Testament. Until now I had been pretty much a layman in matters of literature, but I imagined that no such splendid composition existed elsewhere.

Another thing it showed me was the meaning of 'history'. I sensed that my eyes were opening to the real world. What I saw there was an account of humanity's struggles, its ceaseless wars. Human history is certainly no story of peace. I grasped that the cause of these wars is to be sought in the relationship between man and God. It always comes back to the circumstance that humankind does not know the living and only true God, and is in a state of rebellion against God; in other words it is the reality of human sin which is the cause of wars.

I felt I'd been shown the ultimate problem of humankind. What we had been previously taught as history, in school, was no more than a history of governments. To put it plainly, the recital of historical incidents, but the problem lay more deeply, within human beings themselves. This is what the Bible points out to us. As I thought over this great war, in which the entire world engaged in slaughter, I discerned the foolishness of human beings in ignorance of the true God—their helplessness, and the extent of their unpardonable crimes.

However much the apparent world might progress and develop, outwardly, however high a form might be shown by 20th Century civilisation, the true nature of human beings had not progressed in the least. I could not avoid a sense of boundless wonder that such a book had been written long before the time of Jesus Christ. So the Old Testament became very close and dear to me, considering my fate as a POW. It spanned the gap of the centuries.

With the advent of June, our third winter in the prison camp came round. The place beside the stove again became our favourite spot. By now *go* and *shogi* were no longer as interesting as previously; somehow we couldn't get engrossed in them.

On the other hand, our wishes to study the Bible more deeply increased each day. Padre Troughton seemed to guess our feelings, and wrote away for a series of lessons on doctrine. The theological college in Auckland, from which he'd graduated, issued them as a correspondence course. The outcome was that, at the request of the others, I translated the papers and then gave lectures. This would have been about July; we expected it to take about half a year, and perhaps finish by Christmas.

No forecast could predict when the war would end, but it looked like continuing at least for the rest of the year. For a set period each day the ping-pong table in the recreation room turned into a desk, with us spread around it, happy to carry on with our studies. During these periods we acquired some sort of general outline of the Christian faith.

At last, as the signs came thick and fast that the war was nearing its finale, many of the men became emotionally restless, unable to settle to anything. It seemed the only thing on their minds was worrying about what day the war would end. In the midst of all this, faith gave us the strength to continue to tread the earth firmly and with assurance, without being perplexed about what would happen. The outside turmoil could not reach through to agitate my inner self. I faced each day by seeking the meaning of eternal things, and learnt to be satisfied.

Okinawa and Iwojima fell, and the Japanese mainland became a battlefield. Bombing attacks against the mainland by large formations of B-29 planes increased in severity. The Americans showed the immeasurable might of their material resources, displaying audacity by attacking the homeland everywhere, even with carrier-borne planes from their task forces. It was reported that they were using ships' guns against shore targets.

This news came daily in the English-language newspapers, and they also mentioned the dear names of Japanese cities. The belief in the indestructible land of the gods was shaken to the core by the scientific nature of modern warfare. In the Hawaiian newspapers, they published an aerial photograph looking right down on Tokyo. To see Japan again, the first time for so many years, of all things in an aerial photograph taken from an enemy plane!

At the end of July the well-known Potsdam Declaration was published in the newspapers and the phrase 'Unconditional Surrender' began to make its unpleasant appearance. The final scene was about to be enacted.

One day early in August, when I went into our cookhouse, several people by the cooking stove stood around a page of an English newspaper, engaged in a lively discussion. Curious, I peered at it, and there first saw the words 'atomic bomb' headlined. This was what they had been talking about. We had no knowledge of such things, and could not believe it at first. Hiroshima and then Nagasaki had been obliterated. Whatever the reasons and whatever the circumstances, this was an excessive thing to do against non-combatants. But as we didn't know the dreadful facts, we could not respond to the news with any real feeling.

Meanwhile the newspapers announced that the Soviet Union had entered the Pacific war; it came home to us that at last the final stage had arrived for Japan. The names of many prominent Japanese personalities appeared in the headlines, and we expected the Potsdam Declaration to be accepted that day or the next.

It was still early morning when sirens again reverberated from Featherston, wailing as if they would go on forever. This was the most moving moment of our lives in the prison camp. Without argument and without conditions, the feeling of 'peace' revived in my heart; a sense of blessed relief took control of me. Dare I allow myself to think...is the war all over now? Will humans no longer meet just to kill each other?

The coming of peace! The restoration of peace! I had never before so keenly relished the feeling. If humankind—those presently alive—would never forget that moment, a world war should never break out again. I also felt deep sorrow that our dear country had been beaten in war. But on this occasion, surpassing victory or defeat, the overwhelming emotion was relief that this hateful war had ended.

So the world came back to life again and the state of global war vanished from the earth. As far as Japan was concerned, what had the war finally brought us? Hadn't it all been pointless? You could say that the only outcome was the sacrifice of several million valuable lives, and the destruction of the country. The tragic and sinful nature of war cannot be overstated. For all that, though it might be imagined that a few ignorant and headstrong leaders were the cause, I could not attribute it only to them. I got the painful feeling that the whole nation must accept responsibility and recognise the truth.

This convinced me that Japan must change, taking the opportunity presented by defeat. It must be reborn. If it wasn't, the defeat would be totally without meaning; the countless sacrifices and losses would lose all significance. I even felt that it would be better for Japan to perish utterly, rather than for the Japanese people to let the old ways hold sway. Most important, Japan had to develop a wider view of the world.

When one considered Japan's thousands of years of tradition, it was obvious that this would be no easy matter. Where should we find a basis for rebirth? The more I pondered, the more I was convinced that the Japanese must throw away false human notions and foolish prejudices, and turn humbly to the truths of the Bible. Above all they must learn and accept the true meaning of history as indicated in the Old and New Testaments.

Following the unconditional surrender of Japan on 15 August, the Allied armies (under the command of General MacArthur) began their progressive occupation of Japan, the details of which came to us through newspapers and magazines. The post-surrender condition of the homeland, as seen through the eyes of foreign journalists, became clear. In early September the formal signing of unconditional surrender was enacted on board the American battleship *Missouri* in Tokyo Bay. Now photographs of occupied Japan accompanied newspaper items, ever so dear to us.

Many of the POWs were preoccupied with concerns about their return to Japan. Their heads were so full of it that they generally existed in a state of abstraction. Everything was based on suppositions about 'after we get back to Japan...' with all staked on the day of physical liberation. Considering our present state such thoughts were not unreasonable, but I couldn't help wondering whether true freedom was found in this way. They were obsessed by the idea that there was no freedom until they were liberated from captivity.

But this was not so. This would be no more than simple physical liberation; purely a matter of the external man taking no account of deeper inner freedom. What I wanted to say was that in reality we had actually experienced true freedom only when were held physically captive. When we recognised our own limits we discovered genuine liberation. I believe that freedom is epitomised by the release from sin that is granted through Jesus Christ.

All in all, perhaps our present state was preferable to the day of release, because when surrounded by a barbed wire stockade I came up against my own limits. But in compensation for that, I was sustained with unfailing vitality by the true freedom which is in Jesus Christ. Naturally, as a human being, I preferred the big outside world to the inside of a dry and uninteresting compound. But how would things be when we were released? I knew my weaknesses better than anyone else. Perhaps on the day of release, external freedom would see me pursuing instinctive desires again, which would inevitably lead to my losing true freedom. This remained a paradox right until the last. It saddened me that so many men sought only external freedom, never considering in depth where they were heading.

Although the war had ended, we did not know immediately when we would leave New Zealand for repatriation. I wanted to cherish each day until our release as something truly precious and never to be repeated. The meetings to study doctrine, commenced in July, carried on quietly through until the end of November, when we finally completed the course.

Our prison camp surroundings had already greeted their third advent of spring, with nature at work in the neighbouring pastures. This year too we had a fine crop of strawberries to begin the season. In our compound the solitary double-flowered cherry tree's pale blossoms were twice as plentiful as the previous year. All kinds of flowering plants, as well as tomato, cucumber, and other vegetables, had been planted and were maturing. The topic of speculation amongst us was whether we would be at the camp long enough to enjoy them.

What would be the date of our departure? Already many rumours flew around, centring on this question, which gave a fine insight into human psychology. At first they were all pretty wide of the mark but, as the days passed, the date gradually became firm. The final decision was that two American landing ships (LSTs) would provide transportation, and they were already in Wellington Harbour, being prepared for our accommodation.

The year 1945 was running out, and we celebrated our third and final Christmas in New Zealand.

We continued with our weekly Bible sessions. At each meeting, before the Padre spoke, we took turns to share our thoughts on a Bible text which had specially impressed us. Near Christmas it was my turn.

I read Isaiah Chapter 11; not only did I consider this passage appropriate for Christmas, but also in it I found a text most fitting for our current state of mind.

> There will be a highway for the remnant of his people that is left from Assyria, as there was for Israel when they came up from Egypt.
> Isaiah 11:16

At last the time was close for us to return home after three years in captivity. I could see in my mind's eye a chart drawn of the ocean, and on this chart was the 'highway' of our return home, clearly drawn as a thick sea route uniting New Zealand and Japan.

The exact date of our departure was announced as 30 December, drawing the year to its close; there were only a few days left. Having reached this point, I felt some regret at the farewell. On the one hand I rejoiced, but on the other hand there was a sense of insecurity.

Just over three years had passed since the *Akatsuki* sinking on 13 November 1942. When said in one breath, three years doesn't sound long, but the period spent in New Zealand had been unique. During this interval the world had greatly changed and my life underwent a decisive transformation.

As a POW, I experienced an almost unbearable mental turmoil, a black anguish of immeasurable depth. But as the outcome of this suffering and despair, I found the Bible. I had been touched by the gospel of the cross of Jesus Christ, and had become one able to live by this truth. Now I felt only deep gratitude towards God's boundless grace and God's love shown in the cross of Christ.

In those three years I experienced two great changes. Firstly, becoming a POW, and secondly, becoming a Christian. Neither of these would I ever have dreamt of previously. From prisoner-of-war, to prisoner of Christ. Taking these three years as a significant passage, the course of my life had recorded two great curves.

A few days before we left New Zealand, I noted down three things in simple words in the back of a notebook:

- If a man strives only to live, he will die; if he is prepared to die, he shall live.
- Water settles at its lowest level. Be humble and gentle.
- Love will never come to an end.

These three things could be called my final summation gained from captivity.

Take the first. After the ship sunk, my initial problem was that of dying. I faced the serious and naked confrontation of death and found myself unprepared for it. In turn, I became strongly conscious of the instinct for life as something actively and seriously affecting me. In the end, I found the ultimate solution to this in the death and resurrection of Jesus Christ, but meanwhile I learnt one thing—that only when we are face to face with death do we learn to live in the truest way.

In this sense, life in a POW camp might be called beneficial, because one doesn't know what will happen tomorrow. The prisoner faces continual uncertainty about when he will die. Like a fish on a chopping board, one's life and death are not in one's own hands.

Now I was to be set free; there would be no interference from others, and I would be left alone to lead my life. As a result, this consciousness of death would gradually fade. But would this mean that I would forget how to live in the true sense, and would really die? I could not help being aware of instinctive human weakness, a problem which would arise from my day of liberation.

The second thing I had learnt was humility. Having lived in captivity, the problems I ultimately faced were human limits and finiteness. The individual's instinct to have his own way and expand his own sphere can only crash against a blank wall. I discerned the smallness and weakness of the human creature, and witnessed his lowest depth—things I had been totally unaware of in more favourable times.

It is a great truth that water becomes calm only after it has flowed to its lowest point. During my time in captivity, when I could sink no lower, I first became aware of personal weakness, transience and ugliness. But in the end, when I learnt to be calm at these lower depths, I gained true and unimaginable peace. I was forced to be naturally humble and gentle. And when halfway through I couldn't give myself up entirely, I couldn't attain anything. I found the most ideal example of humility in the life of Jesus Christ leading to the cross.

Finally, the third of these things is that called love, which is the greatest of the three.

Since taken prisoner, the world had become utterly incomprehensible. I fell into deep doubt over such questions as, why do people live? Where is the basis for human life? What are the things of greatest worth? I groped in the dark for lasting concepts of value. And at last I found love.

I remember experiencing a few times the love shown to me by others while I was a POW. And nearly every time this had been by Christian believers. Winding up my accounts for three years, I asked myself what debts remained. What came to mind was really quite minor, but these actions of love stood out. Everything else was pretty well gone and forgotten. I had learned that love given in the name of Jesus Christ is eternal, imperishable, and of the greatest worth. 'Love never fails.' (1 Corinthians 13:8). And, '...now these three remain: faith, hope and love. But the greatest of these is love.' (1 Corinthians 13:13).

Tomorrow would be our final day, tomorrow we would leave New Zealand. We had been nearly three years shut up in the one compound, incarcerated in a monotonous yet mostly tranquil environment. We had come to feel quite at home in the place, and in a way disinclined to move. We had no way of knowing what might await us in the future; in this we were not without a slight sense of insecurity. Be that as it may, I clung firmly to that certain peace granted only through faith in Jesus Christ, as I trod the path of dreams on my last night in that doghouse so rich in memories.

13

Homecoming

Featherston Prisoner-of-War Camp, 30 December 1945.

We were up before daybreak, getting ready for departure while the stars still sparkled in a clear black sky. Even travelling is simple when you're a POW. After handing in my blankets and other items on loan, all that remained were my clothes and a pocketful of personal effects. Should I throw them away too? I wondered.

After hurriedly finishing our last breakfast in the mess-room, they loaded us into a truck and we set off for the station, back along the road on which we had travelled three years previously. The surroundings gradually grew lighter as we entered Featherston, its deserted streets still asleep in the quiet dawn.

The commandant was already at the station. Before long the party of enlisted men and construction workers arrived on foot. While waiting for the train, my eyes lit on the sign FEATHERSTON. I couldn't help gazing at this name and being deeply moved by it. Take a map of the world: there in the southern hemisphere is Australia, and in the sea to the east is New Zealand, a small country of no great note to people in places as Japan. And even less noticeable, this out-of-the-way country town of Featherston. Who on earth had even heard of it? The fact that during the Second World War there had been a Japanese POW camp might become no more than a tale of the past handed down by a few people. But this small town had brought a decisive change to my life, making it a place I would never forget.

With a stirring blast on its steam whistle, the train, specially provided for our transport, drew into the station. At the command of our escort we all piled in. Time marched on relentlessly, leaving no time for pondering on the past, as we set off at a moderate pace.

"Featherston—Sayonara!"

When we arrived we came through Auckland in the north, but on our return we left from the capital city, Wellington, about three hours away by train. The new landscape unrolling outside the carriage window made us quickly forget the past, and turned our thoughts to what lay ahead.

In due time the train pulled into Wellington. The mountains crowded close to the shore with houses strung out halfway up their flanks. The train entered an area like marshalling yards, a tangle of railway tracks. The whole train was switched on to another track and proceeded quietly through to a wharf.

Two American Navy LSTs were tied up alongside the wharf in front of us, with sailors aboard them engaged in duties. It was my first sight of the sea for three years, and what sweet memories it brought. To my mind the sea was my old home. The rippling harbour was reminiscent of that at Etajima, although the seawater was leaden and not very clear.

They immediately led us off the train and on board the LSTs. A cheerful young ensign giving directions led us to a hatchway at the bow of our ship. We instantly sensed an atmosphere of hostility on the part of the crew towards us, stronger than our attitude towards them, perhaps because their impressions of the war zone were still vivid and strong.

Once down below the forward hatch, we officers were put in a compartment on the starboard side below the upper deck. It consisted of three tiers of simple bunks, about 15, attached to the walls on either side, leaving the centre as an access. There were no portholes at all, no glimpse of sea, thus giving one the uncomfortably oppressive sensation of suddenly entering a confined space. The compartment immediately to the rear was used to accommodate twenty or so sick patients. The main body of the enlisted men were put in a wide area in the bottom of the ship intended for carrying motor vehicles and tanks.

Our last farewell salutes were exchanged with the commandant, who had specially come to see us on our way, and with Dr Bossard of the Swiss Red Cross Society and the escorting soldiers. Our hour of departure must have been imminent, for there was some sense of haste. As a final

124

thought Padre Troughton gave us some words of cheer, saying he would send us on our way with the 27th Psalm, from the Old Testament. The ship left port soon after.

When the ship began to toss, we guessed we were out in the open ocean.

From evening the ship's movements became more violent, tending to damp our spirits as we lay miserably wrapped in our blankets. K-rations (field ration packs) were handed round as our evening meal, but we had no appetite for them.

Lying on my bunk, I opened the Bible and read the 27th Psalm.

The LORD is my light and my salvation—
　　whom shall I fear?
The LORD is the stronghold of my life—
　　of whom shall I be afraid?
When evil men advance against me
　　to devour my flesh,
when my enemies and my foes attack me,
　　they will stumble and fall.
Though an army besiege me,
　　my heart will not fear;
though war break out against me,
　　even then will I be confident.

One thing I ask of the LORD,
　　This is what I seek:
that I may dwell in the house of the LORD
　　all the days of my life,
to gaze upon the beauty of the LORD
　　and to seek him in his temple.
For in the day of trouble
　　he will keep me safe in his dwelling;
he will hide me in the shelter of his tabernacle
　　and set me high upon a rock.
Then my head will be exalted
　　above the enemies who surround me;
at his tabernacle will I sacrifice with shouts of joy;
　　I will sing and make music to the LORD.

Hear my voice when I call, O LORD;
 be merciful to me and answer me.
My heart says of you, 'Seek his face!'
 Your face, LORD, I will seek.
Do not hide your face from me,
 do not turn your servant away in anger;
 you have been my helper.
Do not reject me or forsake me,
 O God my Saviour.
Though my father and mother forsake me,
 the LORD will receive me.
Teach me your way, O LORD;
 lead me in a straight path
 because of my oppressors.
Do not turn me over to the desire of my foes,
 for false witnesses rise up against me,
 breathing out violence.

I am still confident of this:
 I will see the goodness of the Lord
 in the land of the living.
Wait for the LORD;
 be strong and take heart
 and wait for the LORD.

The tossing of the ship was pretty violent for a while, but I managed not to be seasick, and the following day the sea calmed. The sun shone and there was no longer any sight of land.

The dawn of New Year's Day 1946 greeted us out on the Pacific Ocean. To be sure, there was no great New Year feeling about it.

Twice each day, morning and afternoon, we were given time in the open air to freshen up; these times out of the confined cabin were our sole pleasure. We could breathe our fill of fresh air and gaze at the boundless blue sky and the deep-blue sea. I could never tire of this sight. Our speed was about 10 knots, painfully slow, but when I considered that every day Japan grew closer I felt my heart swell, although some anxieties still lingered.

Our voyage continued, uneventful and blessed by fine weather...

As our latitude approached the equator the inclination of the sun grew higher, and in proportion my shadow on the upper deck grew gradually shorter. About now we learnt that our first port of call would be Guadalcanal. We knew the ship had entered the tropics because, with our cabin being immediately below the upper deck, the steel plates became scorching hot. To make matters worse there wasn't a single porthole, so it sweltered inside.

The electric ventilator fan in the cabin worked continually, but was pretty ineffective. With evaporation of body moisture I became tired sooner than expected. It was quite impossible to have any sort of bath, and all one could manage was an occasional rub down with water. Our food was one K-ration for each meal, and boiled white rice once every two days. However convenient these field rations may have been, their monotony was hard to endure, particularly so because the heat killed our appetite. All we wanted to do was drink lots of plain water.

After more than ten days at sea, word came that we had arrived at Guadalcanal. I hurried up on deck. The large island loomed off starboard, while astern to port lay small Savo Island. Further in the distance, the islands of Florida and Malaita showed hazily. The whole extent of Guadalcanal Island was mantled in dense jungle, asleep in ominous stillness. I could not avoid a wave of emotion at seeing it again.

The ship sailed on much the same course as that taken by *Akatsuki* during the battle when she'd been sunk. The surrounding islands and everything else were just as they had been then. The world of men had undergone many violent transformations while the world of nature remained ever unchanged. And coming now on this scene, the picture of tranquillity, one tried to imagine why those dreadfully violent battles to the death between Japanese and American forces had occurred on these waters, in that jungle, and under this sky. If my memory was not mistaken, more than 80 ships from Japan, America and other nations lay wrecked on the sea floor. Indeed, the Americans named the area Iron Bottom Sound because so many warships were sunk within sight of the island. The ship sailed on quietly into those same waters.

I suddenly realised that right beneath the course of the ship was the sunken *Akatsuki*. A solemn feeling struck me, inexpressible in words and dreadfully painful, that I would pass directly over that place. The sea's face rippled, heedless as ever.

We could see a Japanese transport ship run aground on the shore, lying as it had been abandoned, displaying its red rusting bottom. It was a stark memento of war.

The ship rounded Lunga Point, near Henderson Airfield, and tied up alongside a hurriedly constructed wharf of sturdy timber. A large transport ship of the wartime type was tied up along one side and some of the local inhabitants worked on board. I drank in the scene, for I had never dreamt that I would see Guadalcanal again.

After staying only one night, we left early the next morning. Our two LSTs made their way up the line of the Solomon Islands, passing through memorable waters we had sailed several times before. It remained windless and the heat was especially severe. Once when we came up on deck, we spotted New Georgia close by on the port side. Later again, the high mountains of Bougainville could be seen, and the ship changed course towards the north, heading for the island of Guam, our next port of call.

Here we crossed the equator and entered the northern hemisphere once more. Our journey this far had seemed exasperatingly slow, with the days so drawn out, but looking at it now it was as though we covered half the voyage in next to no time. The journey continued in the unending heat and dead calm of those windless latitudes.

In time we made port at the island of Guam. It was my first time there. Immediately after arriving we were allowed out on the upper deck, and I ran my eyes attentively over the new sights. I could only stare in amazement at the harbour facilities, which must have been rapidly extended during the war into a significant naval and military base. A large artificial breakwater was under construction and almost completed, with a busy traffic of trucks carrying large rocks.

Inwards from the harbour mouth was an airfield on slightly rising ground, with planes taking off and landing, and a row of camouflaged semi-cylindrical buildings.

An aircraft carrier was anchored in the harbour, possibly a 27,000 ton class built during the war. Several destroyers of a recent type, which we didn't recognise, also lay at anchor with various small ships. Tied up by the breakwater were several LSTs; I imagined they'd probably arrived after taking part in landing operations at places like Okinawa and Iwojima. Also a large floating dock could be seen further in. All this hammered home America's enormous industrial strength, so utterly beyond the ordinary comprehension of us Japanese. Even the Yamato Spirit—that unique and essential Japanese spirit capable of all bravery and overcoming obstacles—had no chance against this.

Yet what shook us more than anything else was spotting a Japanese destroyer among the American ships. Its gun turrets and other armaments had been stripped. Red rising-sun disks had been painted on the hull, apparently for identification. It was probably being used as a demobilisation transport for Japanese troops. Debased and broken, it gave us our first real sense of Japan's defeat.

Towards evening a large plane flew leisurely past. A good look convinced me that it must be a B-29, the first I had seen. I stared at it intently, realising this was the type of plane which had laid waste the principal cities of Japan.

After leaving Guam our next port of call was Chichijima in the Ogasawara Islands. Several small American ships were anchored in the narrow harbour there, while the flag waving over the former Japanese Navy seaplane headquarters was no longer our Naval Ensign but the Stars and Stripes.

A large wireless mast on the hillside looked as though it had suffered a direct hit, knocked completely over and presenting a pitiful sight. Many fishing boats were anchored over by the shore on the right.

We stopped only a few hours at Chichijima, and soon left port. It had seemed a long and tedious voyage so far, but at last the next stop would be our own dear home country. How would it have changed? All sorts of wild imaginings galloped through my brain. We had passed through the torrid zone near the equator, and now set course due north towards Japan, then in the depths of winter. The ship grew cooler daily as we entered higher latitudes, and the temperature steadily dropped.

When only a short way from home, the ship struck its first severe storm. The tossing grew ever wilder. There was dreadful jarring—just when we imagined the ship might come through, it would suddenly plunge its head down again. The almighty force of water smashing against the bow made the hull creak strangely. Considering the ship had a cavernous interior, it seemed the hull was flexing. With our cabin relatively well forward, this seemed particularly ominous. We could do nothing as we listened to the terrible battering of the sea. Long hours passed as we lay on our bunks anxiously wondering when the storm would die down.

Nevertheless the weather gradually improved, and I shaved off a several-weeks-old beard. We'd had about a month of this; with only

K-rations for meals and the terribly hot weather, my eyes were quite sunken. My first look in a mirror for a month showed a face I scarcely recognised. With the realisation that tomorrow we'd be back in Japan, I could hardly sleep.

"Home in sight!"

When I heard this call the next morning, I leapt out of my bunk and rushed up on deck as though propelled by a spring. It was overcast, with the sea still running. An icy winter wind caressed my cheeks as I gazed towards land.

To starboard stretched the familiar long coastal profile of the Boso Peninsula. At its left extremity was the white-walled Nojimazaki Lighthouse. No doubt about it, this was Japan—beautiful land of islands. I swung my eyes further round to port as Oshima and its islands lifted their heads above the horizon. So my native land as seen from the sea presented the same picture, not the least changed these several years.

'The country is broken, the mountains and rivers remain.' This line by the poet Tu Fu sprung immediately to mind. I had never felt the words so vividly. We would set foot again in our home country, now much destroyed by thorough bombing from the American Air Forces, but the world of nature at least presented a sight unaltered.

On 3 February 1946 our two LSTs completed their long voyage of over a month, and dropped anchor off Uraga.

The pale winter sun filtered down on the calm sea as we on deck gazed untiringly at the scene on shore. The Uraga Shipyard dock was just as it used to be, further up the inlet, but the Stars and Stripes waved on the waterfront. The old Japanese Navy small aircraft carrier Hosho was anchored close by, now bringing home troops for demobilisation. American military transport ships passed through the entrance to Tokyo Bay. Planes flew, but these too were American. We faced our first sharp contact with the transformed state of Japan, and the reality of defeat.

That afternoon we finally set foot on Japanese soil. I had visited Uraga many times in the past, but what particularly caught my eye that day was the great many air-raid shelter caves dug in the clay on either side of the road.

We walked to the former Naval Construction School at Kurihama, which had been converted into troop quarters for demobilisation.

Our military release procedures started and the state of our home became apparent from the sights and sounds around us. We were surprised that the people were not as undernourished as we'd presumed; their faces showed no serious signs of suffering in spite of the defeat. But most unexpected was the way prices had shot up to an impossible extent.

On the 6th we were demobilised and thrown into the wide world.

Bundled up in civilian clothes with bulging packs on our shoulders, we got on the Yokosuka Electric Railway at Kurihama Station. The filthy state of the railway carriage amazed us.

Before long the electric train arrived at Yokosuka. The fence, which previously hid the Yokosuka Naval Base from the general public, had been completely removed and the base appeared unchanged.

The train travelled through Zushi and Kamakura; being familiar places made them especially memorable. The sights seen through the carriage window showed less evidence of war damage than I'd expected. Perhaps things wouldn't be so bad, after all.

But after we branched to the right at Ofuna and approached Yokohama, the scene suddenly changed. Bomb damage became clearly visible. As we got closer to Tokyo this became still more dreadful; it was just one great scorched plain, thoroughly done over. There were no signs of restoration at all. Nothing remained except burnt-out ruins. Here and there tombstones dotted cemeteries, looking like clusters of quartz crystals. Turning from the signs of extensive war damage, both sides of the tracks, to the expressionless faces of my fellow passengers, I felt my heart grow hot. One thing came immediately to mind. I exclaimed to myself "The Gospel!" My heart lit with boundless thoughts of love for my defeated country and my countrymen.

The electric train went on through Tsurumi and Kawasaki, crossed the steel bridge over the Rokugo River, and entered Tokyo. Complete destruction spread in all directions.

Before long we pulled into Shinbashi; here our small group of officers alighted. When I gazed towards Atago Hill, there was no longer anything to be seen but a burnt-out plain, and I couldn't imagine that my former home had been spared. We went to the former Ministry of the Navy, where our final procedures were concluded. These over, we went at last our separate ways, each taking his own road home.

My home in Shiba, as I feared, had been completely destroyed in the wartime fires so I went on to my older sister's house in Ushigome. It had been miraculously spared from damage. Here I learnt the latest news of my family. Happily, both my parents and younger brother were safe in a reception area in Yokohama.

My homecoming was like the return of a ghost. My family had given up hope of my survival and my funeral rites had been conducted. So the family was united again. My friends and family welcomed me back from the dead, and I had somewhere to settle down.

I had to sit still for a while, to fill up the void of the missing three years and to adapt myself to social conditions in the defeated country. One question preoccupied me. What should I do next? It was the time of changeover to the new Yen. Society was troubled by inflation, foodstuffs were in short supply, on every hand instability and unrest simmered; it was a chaotic situation, the future unpredictable. Just living each day was a difficult enough business.

In the middle of all this, I was desperate to enter a theological college and devote myself to study, to respond to the mission that God sent me. But when I carefully considered the situation, the idea seemed thoughtless and extravagant. It seemed better to plunge straight away into the community, to work there while living for the Gospel of Jesus Christ.

I felt that I was falling short of devoting my whole life to Jesus Christ's calling. But on the other hand, I could hardly abandon my family. The dilemma tortured me until, believing in God's guidance, a fortunate opportunity allowed me to enrol in the Japan Biblical Seminary at Mejiro in Tokyo. This fulfilled my most earnest prayer and allowed to respond to the calling that I had received in the New Zealand POW camp.

As I stood amidst the ruins of my beloved country, I recognised my wartime experiences made me love Japan more wisely and more deeply. I could not see what the future held. All I could be sure of was a divine love that burned within bringing with it the knowledge that beyond death and dishonour new life emerges.

Epilogue to the Wounded

Three years later, after completing my studies, I was granted a position serving the Kanuma and Utsunomiya Churches in Toshigi Prefecture, both belonged to the United Church of Christ in Japan. So it was that I took my first steps in the work of spreading the Gospel, and proclaiming the Bible's message from the sacred pulpit.

In 1980 I returned to New Zealand for the first time with my wife and daughter. I visited the site of the Featherston Camp and meet up with some of the New Zealanders who had been involved in camp life.

Looking back, despite the incident of 25 February 1943, we had really been treated very well by our captors all those years ago. After the war it became clear that Japanese forces had not been hospitable to the prisoners which they held. I want to sincerely express my deep apology to those ill-treated soldiers and their families for the atrocities which were committed on them by my countrymen.

The ethic which we held in those years about the superiority of the Japanese race, and the unsurpassed shame of being taken prisoner, meant that we had little respect for foreign prisoners or the worth of an individual.

But through my experiences at Featherston and my encounter with Christianity, I learnt that we are all brothers and sisters beyond the barrier of nations, races and colours. We can forgive each other, and love each other, through faith in Jesus Christ.

Please forgive our atrocities during the war. I know there is still much pain, but I deeply hope there will be reconciliation among us all.

Michiharu Shinya, April 2001.

Appendices

Appendix I

Translator's Notes

A personal note from the translator

In May–August 1943 I was one of five soldiers sent by the New Zealand Army to Featherston POW Camp, to be student-interpreters, with the rank of sergeant. We were soldiers who had shown some interest in learning Japanese, or who were otherwise presumed to have an aptitude for the language. We had Japanese instructors who came out daily from the enlisted men's compound, and did not have much contact with most of the inmates of the officers' compound.

I remember how, soon after first arriving in Featherston, on about June 1943, I went on the rounds once with the duty officer for the day. I remember the duty officer (whoever it may have been) stopped where some kind of shrine had been built by the Japanese at the corner of a compound, apparently in memory of those who had died in the 25 February Incident. While we stood by, he marched up to it, halted, saluted, about-faced, and marched back the few paces to where we were, before going on with his rounds. At Featherston in March 1974 (31 years later) I hunted in vain for any trace of this shrine or cairn.

I also remember, on that occasion in 1943, going on with the duty officer into the Japanese officers' compound. Here my memory plays tricks with me, but I seem to remember one older slightly more genial Japanese officer (probably Senior Lieutenant Kamikubo) standing to attention and exchanging a few words with the New Zealand officer. I also think that I remember one young Japanese officer with a pale and vacant look, gazing blankly into space, and like to think that I remember Shinya-san, and how he gave me some cause for thought.

Eric Thompson

1. The author

The author, Mr Michiharu Shinya, was born in 1920 in Tokyo, and graduated from the Japanese Naval Academy at Etajima, the Japan Biblical Seminary in Tokyo, and McCormick Theological Seminary in Chicago. He later became Principal of the Japan Biblical Seminary, one of the theological colleges of the United Church of Christ in Japan (the Nippon Kirisuto Kyodan), and was concurrently Pastor of the Akebono Church, in Tokyo.

In a postscript to the 1957 Japanese edition of this book (*Shi no Umi yori Kodan e*) Michiharu Shinya wrote how back in the days when he was a theology student, soon after the war, he used to visit his teacher of Greek, a Mr Toshiro Suzuki, at Kamakura. On one occasion the teacher mentioned how Pastor Martin Niemoller had written in his life story about having previously been a German naval officer. This lit the idea in Mr Shinya's mind of writing his own story some day.

In 1949, after he had graduated from theological seminary, Mr Shinya served four years as pastor for the Kanuma and Utsunomiya Churches in Tochigi Prefecture. Articles that he wrote at that time for a monthly church bulletin, entitled 'From a Destroyer to the Pulpit', formed the bones of this present book. He had prepared the draft on the side during continuing preaching and pastoral work, but did not find an opportunity then for further publication.

While pastor at these churches, Mr Shinya also served as a lecturer at his former college, the Japan Biblical Seminary. Then after selection in an examination conducted by the United Church of Christ in Japan, he spent over four years in the United States on theological studies, mainly in the Old Testament field; he studied under Professors G. Ernest Wright and F. M. Cross Jr at McCormick, from which he graduated Master of Theology.

While in Chicago Mr Shinya spent some time as minister of the local Japanese Presbyterian and Methodist churches. It was those he met then who encouraged him to complete the first edition of his wartime story for its publication in Japanese in 1957. He attended the Second Assembly of the World Council of Churches at Evanston in 1954, at the nomination of the United Church of Christ in Japan, and there was able to hear and meet Pastor Niemoller.

Upon returning from America, Mr Shinya served at the Japan Biblical Seminary in Tokyo as a professor, and in 1973 became Principal.

In March 1987, Mr Shinya retired from his position as Principal of the Japan Bible Seminary.

In July and August 1992, Mr Shinya was invited with his wife to take part in the underwater investigation carried out by the National Geographic Society of America, of ships sunken in the waters around Guadalcanal. During this time, Mr Shinya met Mr H.S. Moredock and Mr Bert Warne from *Atlanta* and *Canberra* respectively—allied ships sunk during the naval battle in which *Akatsuki* was lost.

In March 1996, Mr Shinya retired from church ministry, and in June of that year travelled to America to meet Mr Gunterman, a sailor aboard U.S.S. *Zane*—one of the ships which engaged *Akatsuki* off Guadalcanal.

Mr Shinya's published works include his Bible commentaries on Deuteronomy and 1 and 2 Chronicles, and translations of works by G. Ernest Wright (*God Who Acts*), T.H. Kuist (Jeremiah, and Lamentations), N. H. Snaith (a joint translation of *The Distinctive Ideas of the Old Testament*), and John Bright (*History of Israel*).

Mr Shinya currently lives with his wife in Yokohama and has two sons, one daughter and three grandchildren.

2. Guadalcanal

The name 'Guadalcanal' is Spanish. The island was first seen by Europeans in 1568 when the two small sailing ships *Los Reyes* and *Todos Santos*, commanded by Alvaro de Mendana, nephew of the Viceroy of Peru, came westwards looking for gold where it was supposed the Land of Ophir—'the Islands of King Solomon'—might be found. The Spaniards met warlike 'Indians' there, and blood was shed on both sides.

The Americans shed much more blood in 1942 around where the town of Honiara now stands and around the airfield originally constructed by the Japanese but enlarged and named Henderson Field by the Americans.

The remaining Japanese on Guadalcanal were finally driven up to the north-west corner of the island, from where some 12,000 were evacuated, slipping away by night early in February 1943. Guadalcanal was as far as the Japanese ever got on land in their 1942 advances in the Pacific, and it remained to them a memory of terrible efforts and tragic failure.

Savo Island stands sentinel a few miles off Cape Esperance at the north-west corner of Guadalcanal, and was the pivot of several naval battles. The Americans called it 'The Battle of Savo Island' when the Japanese Navy made its first counterstroke during the night of 8–9 August 1942, sinking the Allied heavy cruisers *Astoria*, *Quincy*, *Vincennes*, and *Canberra*. Then they gave the name 'Battle of Cape Esperance' to the night battle of 11–12 October, when *Furutaka* and the destroyer *Fubuki* were sunk, and Rear Admiral Aritomo Goto aboard the *Aoba* was among those killed.

When the big climax came in the three night sea battle of 12–15 November 1942, it became 'The Naval Battle of Guadalcanal'. *Akatsuki* was not the only casualty that first night. The Americans had only cruisers and destroyers to put against the Japanese battleships, but some of their ships were equipped with early types of radar. The opposing ships intermingled at close range in the darkness, sometimes firing on friend as well as foe. Several hundred Americans were killed, including their two admirals—Rear Admiral Daniel J. Callaghan in the heavy cruiser *San Francisco* and Rear Admiral Norman Scott in the anti-aircraft cruiser *Atlanta*. Four American destroyers (*Barton*, *Monssen*, *Cushing*, and *Laffey*) were sunk. *Atlanta* was burnt out with many dead and was so badly damaged that it had to be scuttled late the next day near Lunga Point; this must have been the ship seen by our author shortly after his capture. A torpedo from a submarine sank its sister ship *Juneau* while retiring from the battle. These two ships were of 6000 tons, each with sixteen 5 inch dual-purpose guns. The heavy cruiser *Portland* had its stern plates buckled by a torpedo during the night battle, so that it could only cruise in circles until assisted, and must have been the one seen by the author.

The Japanese also had their losses. The destroyers *Akatsuki* and *Yudachi* were sunk; their flagship *Hiei* was so badly damaged that it had to be scuttled late the next day, with survivors being taken off by other Japanese ships.

The second night (the author's first night as a POW) Japanese cruisers and destroyers shelled the American positions near Henderson Field.

The third night brought the two newly completed American battleships *Washington* and *South Dakota* into the battle. The latter was badly damaged, but *Washington* approached unseen and wrecked the *Kirishima* with a few minutes of radar-controlled fire from its nine 16 inch guns, such that this Japanese battleship too had to be abandoned and survivors taken off.

From *Akatsuki* Captain Yusuke Yamada (Commanding Officer, Sixth Destroyer Division), Commander Osamu Takasuka (Captain of the *Akatsuki*), and Lieutenant Tatsuo Yamagata (Gunnery Officer on the *Akatsuki*) lost their lives.

Yamato and its sister ship *Musashi*, named after the two main ancient provinces of Japan, were at 70,000 tons the two largest battleships (that is big-gunned warships) ever built. Their details were kept secret, and only after the war did their size and the fact that they each had nine 46 cm (18 inch) guns become generally known. Both were sunk by air attack before the end of the war.

The battleships *Kongo*, *Haruna*, *Hiei*, and *Kirishima*, named after notable mountains of Japan, were originally battle-cruisers of 1913–1915 vintage, the prototype *Kongo* being built in Britain and similar to H.M.S. *Tiger*. They had been extensively reconstructed, more heavily protected, and re-engined, emerging as fast battleships of 32,000 tons, 30 knots, and with eight 36 cm (14 inch) guns each. In the early months of the war, ships of this class had escorted the fast aircraft-carriers in their wide-ranging attacks from Pearl Harbour to Colombo.

The *Furutaka*-class cruisers (of the Sixth Squadron) were of some 9000 tons, with six 20 cm (8 inch) guns, equivalent to the British *Exeter* class.

The Japanese destroyers bore poetic sounding names related to natural phenomena, such as *Akatsuki* (Dawn), *Hibiki* (Echo), *Ikazuchi* (Thunder), *Inazuma* (Lightning), *Amagiri* (Sky Mist), and *Takanami* (High Wave). These were ships typically of about 2000 tons, 34 knots, with six 12.7 cm (5 inch) guns in three turrets, and nine 61 cm (24 inch) torpedo tubes.

The Japanese torpedoes on these ships were oxygen-propelled, and more powerful, faster, and of longer range than those of other navies. Although developed in 1933, they remained in effect a secret weapon in 1942–43. This is mentioned in Morison's account (*The Two-Ocean War*) of the Battle of Kolombangara during the night 12–13 July 1943, when two American cruisers (*Honolulu* and *St Louis*) and the New Zealand cruiser *Leander* received torpedo hits. The Japanese aimed their torpedoes with keen eyesight and powerful optical instruments, but their night gunnery required the doubtful expedient of switching on searchlights; they still had no radar in 1942–43.

Nearly twenty years later the Japanese destroyer *Amagiri* was retrospectively awarded a niche in American history: on the night of 1–2 August 1943 off Kolombangara it rammed and sank the American torpedo boat PT-109; commanded by Lieutenant John F. Kennedy.

3. Featherston Camp

In late 1942–1943 a POW camp was constructed on a site on the Wairarapa plain, some three kilometres east of the small town of Featherston, on the north side of the main road to Masterton. There had been a military training camp here during the First World War.

There was some haste about the initial construction, as several hundred Japanese captives were suddenly passed over to the New Zealand military authorities, and many more were expected as the Allied counter-offensive in the Pacific developed. However no more POWs were sent down to New Zealand after the Americans had secured Guadalcanal. This left New Zealand with a more elaborate establishment at Featherston than perhaps necessary, while those Japanese captured during the later campaigns in the Pacific were shipped back along the lines of communication towards the American mainland. Japanese captured in the New Guinea area were sent to a camp at Cowra, New South Wales, in Australia.

Half of the inmates of the Featherston camp were civilian airfield construction workers, and half were from the Japanese armed forces, mainly from the navy. Considering the Japanese aversion to being taken prisoner, it might be doubted whether 200 men would be captured from the sinking of one cruiser. Yet while colder waters would kill quickly, men left floating in the tropics may survive for several days, but enfeebled by exposure to the sun and sea, as well as very likely suffering from wounds and shock, a large number could thus be picked up from one ship if the tactical situation allowed it and if the effort was made. It is on record, for example, in one of the New Zealand official war history volumes (S.D. Waters, *The Royal New Zealand Navy*, 1956) that 78 survivors of the Japanese destroyer *Yugumo* were picked up from the sea by American torpedo boats off Vella Lavella after the night battle of 6–7 October 1943. Some of these wounded Japanese were put in an army hospital on Vella Lavella; there two New Zealand Army sergeants, recently arrived at Third N.Z. Division Headquarters after three months at Featherston learning basic Japanese, had the duty of interrogating them; this was not a very productive effort.

The confrontation and shooting incident of 25 February 1943 leaves its mark on the record. Among other things, it might be asked in retrospect how some 30 New Zealand soldiers, with rifles and sub-machineguns, came to be lined up inside the POW compound more or less within or barely out of rushing distance of 250 or more Japanese, and why the situation should have been let or forced to develop in such a dramatic manner.

During a two-hour confrontation repeated demands were made that the Japanese form and send out working parties, while various physical methods were used to try and extract the Japanese spokesmen. These included two Japanese officers who had been sent or let in that morning to act as intermediaries, but who did not produce the result expected. Lieutenant Nishimura was thus grabbed and hustled back to the officers' compound, but Lieutenant Adachi remained out of reach. Toshio Adachi seems to have been one of the 'moderate faction', but to him now fell the privilege of confronting the camp adjutant Lieutenant J. Malcolm and declaring, before all present, words to the effect that 'I am prepared to die with my countrymen if that is necessary'.

After some warning, Malcolm then shot and wounded Adachi once or more, and the Japanese rose as a body, in anger, and either started to rush or seemed about to rush the line of New Zealand guards. A simple account would state that the POWs rushed at the guards, but some doubt lingers as to whether a really determined and concerted rush by the Japanese would not have covered the small gap between and overwhelmed the guards, in spite of all losses. The death wish and the instinct for life, the way of the warrior and the spark of human hope, their enduring patriotism and the brand of shame, all those things which had been mixed up and clashing in each Japanese heart for many weeks came to a climax at that moment and perhaps brought a fleeting instant of indecision, in spite of all the yells of anger, the throwing of stones, and the surge forward of the mass of the Japanese prisoners.

In any case the New Zealand soldiers, with their own mixed burden of wartime feelings, reacted spontaneously to the dangerous situation they found themselves in. In a 15–30 second burst of firing from some 29 rifles and five Thompson sub-machineguns, 31 Japanese were left dead, 17 more fatally wounded, and about 74 others wounded. One New Zealand officer and five other ranks received gunshot wounds, and one of these later died. These men had been round the other side of the body of Japanese, hit by bullets from their own comrades. Stones wounded one New Zealand officer and nine other ranks. Approximately 70 rounds had been fired from the .45 inch sub-machineguns, and 150 rounds from the .303 inch rifles.

Toshio Adachi recovered, and returned to Japan. Keith Robertson wrote in 1975, 'He is described by all ex-POWs as "*honto ni chumoku-subeki na hito*" (a truly notable man). He regularly tended a monument erected by former *Furutaka* men, in the Kure Naval Cemetery. He has since died.

A military Court of Inquiry reached its conclusions on 13 March 1943. It is understood that the Swiss Consul (representing the Protecting Power) and the Delegate of the International Committee of the Red Cross also reported.

This incident has been referred to as a 'riot' or 'attempted break-out'. We have imagined a disciplined body of Japanese fighting men seizing weapons and stores, breaking out and living off the countryside, hiding in forested gorges, and somehow carrying on the war; this attributes to the Japanese the motives and resources which POWs from some other nation might possibly have had. In truth, these were disgraced and broken men; the officers were equally disgraced and had no formal authority; the great discipline and fighting power of Japanese troops were extinguished from the moment of capture; Japan had no need for POWs to fight its battles.

In the Featherston POW Camp a concrete products factory and a furniture factory were set up, where some of the Japanese worked. Others went out under armed escort to cultivate vegetable gardens in the neighbourhood. Others worked in the hospital, the dental clinic, clothing and shoe workshops, and at camp maintenance, etc. With the large camp establishment it could hardly have been an economic operation, but things settled down on an apparent basis of mutual respect within a short time after the shooting incident. In this, the Japanese who had been wounded were much influenced by the medical care they received. Only a few became Christians, most continued to believe in the rightness of the Japanese cause, but there was a general change of atmosphere well before the end of the war, in some ways a foretaste of the coming post-war changes.

Japanese POWs were issued with New Zealand Army uniforms, including the broad-brimmed felt hats, all dyed black. The uniforms were old First World War style in the early days, but later issues were sometimes Second World War battledress. The Japanese usually wore the hats with a round dish on top, in contrast to the New Zealand soldiers' 'lemon-squeezer' (boy scout) style.

No Japanese POW at Featherston ever wrote a letter home, or received any mail from home, although facilities for this were in principle available through the International Committee of the Red Cross and neutral countries.

Many of the Japanese assumed false names as POWs, to hide their shame and hoping to protect their families back home from ostracism. Some of these assumed names were only adaptations of their real names, while others were quite distinct. The author's assumed surname at Featherston was Kawai.

The camp was dismantled after the war.

Appendix II

The following is a transcript of the letter sent to Rev. Troughton requesting his presence at Featherston POW Camp.

NEW ZEALAND MILITARY FORCES.

HEADQUARTERS,
Central Military District
PO Box 118, Te Aro,
WELLINGTON
6th. May, 1943.

Rev. Troughton,
The Manse,
TUAKAU.

Dear Mr. Troughton,

This letter may be a surprise to you, especially as the writer will be unknown to you, but I have a request to make.

I understand that some time back you were requested to take an appointment as Interpreter (Japanese) at the Prisoners of War Camp, on account of your knowledge of Japanese, and that still later considerable pressure was brought to bear that you would take up an appointment as Y.M.C.A. Secretary at the same Camp, both of which requests you felt unable to comply with.

I now make a request which I am afraid you will be unable to dispose of so easily. Recently Dr. Bossard visited the Prisoners of War Camp and reported as follows:-

"Dr. Bossard was rather surprised at a request from officers and N.C.O.'s (Japanese P.W.) for spiritual advice in connection with the Christian faith. These men are not Christians but wanted to understand our way of life.............."

I feel that this will appeal to you, as you know there are a considerable number of prisoners in Camp and it appears to be in line with the work that at one time you carried out in Japan. I do not know to whom I can turn to fill this request if you are still unavailable, but I feel that you can hardly refuse such a request for the reasons that you have mentioned heretofor.

I would be quite prepared for you to come down here for, say, a month's try-out, at the end of which you could say whether or not you were prepared to continue, if this would help to meet any of your objections.

I would also add that I cannot make an application for authority to so employ you from Army Headquarters, until I have received your reply, and this will be necessary before matters can be finalised. May I ask for your reply to this proposition after your earnest consideration.

Yours faithfully,

COLONEL. N.Z.S.C.
District Commandant.
CENTRAL MILITARY DISTRICT.

Appendix III

The following article was written by Rev. Troughton in 1984 about his time at Featherston POW Camp. The memo he mentions concerning a depressed Japanese POW relates to the author, Michiharu Shinya.

The work of the padre

The outcome of a riot at Featherston POW Camp resulted in a number of prisoners being killed or injured. In hospital the wounded were kindly treated and cared for. Some prisoners wondered if this kindness was because of Christianity and their curiosity led to a request for instruction in the Christian faith.

As I had been involved in missionary work in Japan for over five years, the authorities invited me to enter the camp as a padre working with the prison forces (about 500 in all) and their prisoners. My services commenced on 12 July 1943.

The Japanese were housed in three compounds
1. The officers
2. NCOs and other ranks
3. The labouring corp.

It was possible to visit the compounds with every help and support from the army authorities.

For a while my visits to the compounds involved getting to know the prisoners personally. They appreciated someone who could speak with them in their own language and knew something about their culture.

The first vital contact came in the officers' compound. A naval captain told how his ship was bombed and shelled and how he went down with it.

After some time he came to the surface and felt and believed he was being upheld by a supreme power. So I spoke to him about the true and living God who is the Supreme Power.

This conversation led to a regular Bible study for some of the officers, and before long the captain put his trust in the Lord Jesus Christ. Soon afterwards another officer sought me out saying that he wished to accept the Saviour. This he did and the testimony of these two made a profound impact on the others.

After two more officers professed faith, the group drew up a letter of testimony and asked that it be read in the compounds. Permission was granted and before long, meetings were being held regularly in the camp.

In compound two, a group had been formed that called themselves the 'Harikiri' (Suicide) Squad. They believed that being taken a prisoner-of-war was a disgrace and dishonour to their nation and therefore they should commit suicide. None ever did.

The ringleader of this group came to a few services, but was very indignant to discover that the Bible labelled him a sinner (Romans 3:23). For a time he stayed away, but unexpectedly one evening he reappeared. The study was on the conversion and witness of the Apostle Peter, with a closing reference to 1 John 1:7,9: '...the blood of Jesus, his Son, purifies us from all sin. If we confess our sins, he is faithful and just and will forgive us our sins and purify us from all unrighteousness.'

The next day the duty officer, on his rounds, noticed this agitator addressing a group of his mates. He was holding up a Bible and saying, "This is the best book in the world; everyone should read it." Later when I visited him he told me that after the service he couldn't sleep. The message from 1 John 1:7,9 kept coming back and he could find no rest and peace until he knelt, confessed his sins and believed in the Saviour.

Before this encounter with the Lord he looked on Christians as traitors to their country. He also thought he could never return home to his wife and four children because he was a prisoner-of-war.

What took place was an example of the saving grace of God, and an illustration of what Paul refers to in 2 Corinthians 5:17, 'Therefore, if anyone is in Christ, he is a new creation; the old has gone, the new has come!' Now the officer longed to return home to tell his family and others of his newfound Saviour, and to read through the Bible before returning.

In God's time, which is perfect, we were indebted to the International Red Cross for obtaining for us Japanese Bibles through the New York Bible Society. One of them was given to the cook in the officers' compound who was showing interest. A few days later he came to me holding his Bible and saying, "God told me this is his book."

A day or so later his comment was "This book tells me I'm a sinner." My reaction was "Do you believe that?"

"Yes, I do," he replied.

I referred him to 1 John 1:7,9 and he put his trust in the Saviour and rejoiced in the knowledge that his sins had been forgiven.

Now he faced a problem as he had erected a small god shelf in the cookhouse. But not long afterwards the god-shelf disappeared—perhaps broken up and burned in the copper fire. The newfound love of Christ and satisfaction in him had superseded all else.

There was much evidence of the sovereign work of the Lord in men's lives as aided by the Holy Spirit. Behind the scenes, a number of New Zealand Christians were praying regularly for the camp.

On one occasion a memo was sent out asking us to keep a check on a certain officer. He was very introspective, moody and depressed and it was feared that he might try to take his own life. But around this time he started to show interest in Christian matters, and began to read and study the Bible. In due course he came to a saving faith in the Lord Jesus Christ. The evidence was clear; his depression lifted and he became positive and vital.

Later, the Christian officers asked for more and deeper Bible study, my full program made such a request difficult to fulfil. Instead I felt constrained to obtain from the Bible College of New Zealand one of their study books on Christian doctrine and, to my surprise, the officers chose this recent convert to translate and conduct the studies.

When the prisoners returned to Japan, this officer took theological studies in Tokyo, and later in Chicago. He went on to become the principal of the Japan Bible Seminary in Tokyo, where he was used by God in a strategic setting, training young people for Christian service.

He returned to New Zealand in 1980 with his wife and daughter. It was a great joy and privilege to meet him again and to rejoice together as one in the Lord, sharing an affinity of faith and spirit.

In a TV interview he said, "The first time I came to New Zealand as a POW, this time I come as a prisoner of Jesus Christ."

These are just some of the happenings that took place, and some of the lives changed by the grace of God. The response of POWs to the Christian faith played a vital part in easing tension within the camp, and creating a spirit of goodwill.

These men came down to New Zealand as POWs and in a number of cases they found Christ and began a new life in him. They returned home as ambassadors for Christ, sharing the Christian message and experience with their families and others.

It was the Lord's doing. To God be the glory. All praise be to him.

Hessell W.F. Troughton

Glossary

Barrage Balloons. Anti-aircraft barrier of steel cables supported almost vertically each by a balloon.

Bossard, Leon Emil Jakob. (formerly Bosshard) (1894–1964, b. Zurich, d. Auckland) was a doctor of geology and petrology, and worked on oil prospecting in New Zealand for petroleum companies. He was appointed International Committee of the Red Cross delegate in New Zealand in 1942.

Counsul of Switzerland. The Consul of Switzerland in Wellington from 1937–1946 was Dr Walter Schmid. During the Second World War, Switzerland acted as Protecting Power for a number of countries, that is a neutral government accepted as representing the interests of one belligerent state within the territories of another. The Swiss Consul in Wellington was in charge of German, Japanese, Italian, Siamese, and Bulgarian interests. He inspected the internment and prison camps on a regular basis, had to intervene on several occasions when difficulties arose, and reported via Berne to the mandatory state.

Geisha. Japanese dancing girl.

Go and Shogi. In general terms the oriental equivalents of draughts and chess.

Guadalcanal Volunteer Force. (*Ga-to Teishintai*). The designation 'Guadalcanal Volunteer Force' for this naval task force was apparently a code name, but there may have been some confusion or deliberate double meaning with another Japanese word of the same pronunciation meaning 'raiding force'.

Gunpei Yamamuro. (1872–1940) Joined the Salvation Army in 1895 and established it in Japan.

Heihachiro Togo. (1847–1934) Admiral of the Fleet, Commander in Chief of the Japanese Combined Fleet which destroyed the Russian Baltic Fleet at the Battle of Tsushima (the Battle of the Sea of Japan) in 1905.

Joshu District. The Joshu district is the modern Gunma Prefecture, in the lee of the main mountain chain of Honshu. It is noted for its dry hot submontane winds, and for the sericulture which has given its women a more independent economic status than is usual in Japan.

Kansai. The district centred on Osaka.

Kanto. The Tokyo district.

Kusunoki Masashige. (1294–1336) A warrior and military leader who fought to abolish the power of the Kamakura Shoguns and restore the direct rule of the Emperor. This cause was betrayed by the usurper Ashikaga Takauji, who defeated and killed Kusunoki Masashige at the battle of Minatogawa where Kobe City now stands, and founded the Muromachi Shogunate. Kusunoki Masashige came to be venerated as representing the ideal of loyalty to the Emperor.

LST. (Landing Ship, Tanks) were the largest of the beach landing type of ship developed during the Second World War. They were of about 3000 tons, with superstructure aft; large doors opened at the bow and a ramp swung down.

Minami no Risokyo Nyujiirando. The book *Minami no Risokyo Nyujiirando* was by Isamu Kawase, an agricultural scientist who had spent some time at Canterbury Agricultural College, Lincoln, near Christchurch, before the war. Dr Kawase visited New Zealand again in 1977. A thick paperback of 400 pages, published in Tokyo in August 1941, this book is still probably the best comprehensive account of New Zealand published in Japanese. There is a copy in the Turnbull Library, and an article about it in *The Turnbull Library Record*, May 1976.

Po-Yi and Shu-Ch'i. Ancient Chinese worthies commended by Confucius and Mencius. Sons of the king of a small Chinese state, they declined the throne, retired into obscurity, and finally died of hunger, rather than do what they thought wrong.

Rank—author's. The author's rank was *chu-i*, that is in Japanese terms a lieutenant of the middle grade, comparable to British naval sub-lieutenant and American lieutenant (junior grade). The next senior rank was *tai-i* (senior lieutenant), and more junior was *sho-i* (junior lieutenant).

The Japanese designations of rank were the same for navy and army, with also a single term (*heitai* or *hei*) for ratings or other ranks below petty officer or non-commissioned officer, and including these latter in some contexts. The American term 'enlisted men' is thus used here, and it also distinguishes these enlisted men from the drafted construction workers (*choyo koin*), who did not have military status.

Rickshaw. Light two-wheeled vehicle drawn by men, first used 1870 in Japan.

Rikkyo University. Situated in Tokyo, also known as St Paul's University, founded in 1874 by American missionaries, is a multi-faculty institution affiliated to the Nippon Sei Ko Kai (the Protestant Episcopal Church).

Robert Laidlaw. (1885–1971) Founder of the Farmers Trading Company, Auckland's largest department store. Over 33 million copies, in more than 30 languages, of his book *The Reason Why* have been published. He published a new edition *The Story of the Reason Why* in 1969. A biography of Mr. Laidlaw, *Man for our Time* by Ian Hunter, was published in 1999 by Castle Publishing and includes in its appendix the text of *The Reason Why*.

Roka Tokutomi. (1868–1927) A novelist and essayist, Christian, and admirer of Tolstoy. His partly autobiographical novel *Omoide no Ki* (first published 1901) is in English translation by Kenneth Strong called *Footprints in the Snow* (G. Allen & Unwin, 1970) published as one of the UNESCO Collection of Representative Works. In the translator's preface there is an account of how Roka met Tolstoy. Roka was a pen-name, his real name being Kenjiro Tokutomi.

Seki-ga-hara. The battle of Seki-ga-hara was fought in 1600, and led to the centralised feudal system of the Tokugawa era, which ruled Japan in peace and isolation from the rest of the world for 250 years. It is a by-word in Japanese for a decisive battle.

Society of Friends. The Quaker who visited the author in hospital was probably Donald Whisker (1906–1962). He lived in Carterton during the war years, and from about 1949 in Auckland.

Takeo Hirose. (1868–1904), a naval officer, commander, led the Japanese ships sunk across the entrance to Port Arthur in an attempt to trap the Russian ships there, becoming a Japanese war hero.

Tatami (mats). A traditional Japanese unit of measure of the size of rooms, being a mat about 1.8 m by 0.9 m.

Toyohiko Kagawa. (1888–1960) A prominent Japanese Christian and socialist.

Troughton, Hessel. Trained in 1930–1931 at the Bible Training Institute in Auckland, and served in the Central Japan Pioneer Mission 1934–1939; while in Japan he was at Kobe, Maebashi, and Nagaoka. Since the war he has served in the Presbyterian ministry in New Zealand, at Greytown, Ravensbourne–St Leonards, and Orewa. He has since died.

Tu Fu. (712–770) A Chinese poet.

Yamato. The Yamato Spirit was considered to be that unique and essential Japanese spirit capable of all bravery and overcoming all obstacles.

Thanks for reading a Castle Book

Castle Publishing was established to enable writers to take their dynamic messages and God-given talents to a wide international audience.
We seek to maintain a standard of excellence and innovation in all our published material.
Our projects are dedicated to God, who gave us the vision for this endeavour.

Recent titles by Castle:

Robert Laidlaw—Man For Our Time
By Ian Hunter

Through Blood and Fire—The Life of William Booth
By Trevor Yaxley

Direct Encounter—A Lifetime Adventure
By Joyce Mitchell